'Tony, a much-loved Christian leader, shares with humility his life story, in an easy-to-read narrative. But this is much more than an autobiography. Breaking life and faith into different stages, Tony uses his experiences to help us reflect on our own spiritual journeys. Containing questions to reflect on, *Footsteps of Faith* can be used by individuals and groups to help us better understand ourselves and others. Highly recommended for those who want to grow spiritually.'
Dr Debbie Hawker, clinical psychologist

'Tony is the author that I consistently recommend to Christian friends, missionaries, students and member care workers. This new book will be joining the list of recommendations. It is fascinating to read about the twists and turns of Tony's life, but this is not a blow by blow account of his life. Rather it tells key elements of his story through the reflective lens of God's power and plan. The reflections and questions at the end of each chapter are so helpful in applying Tony's experiences to our own lives. To read it is to feel as though you're chatting to him over a cuppa and you don't want the conversation to end.'
Sarah Hay, HR and member care manager, European Christian Mission, and visiting lecturer, All Nations Christian College

'This book is a generous gift. As Tony reflects on the formative work of the Lord in his life and leadership, he opens a space for us to discern the fingerprints of God in our own story. Reading this book feels like a conversation with a wise and experienced mentor. Whatever stage you're at, his reflections will help you see your journey with deeper clarity and to be more present to the ways of God in what lies ahead.'
Melinda Hendry, ministry development lead, Living Leadership

'*Footsteps of Faith* is an engaging spiritual autobiography of how Tony has learned to both seek and see God through the seasons of his life and ministry in service of Jesus. Tony's desire to teach, disciple and mentor people in their faith in Jesus, to help all of us to more clearly discern God's guidance, is evident throughout the book.'
Cliff Kay, Anglican minister, diocese of Sheffield, UK

'One of the profound gifts in life is to learn from others who are further on the journey than ourselves. Tony offers this valuable gift. This is a brilliant book, rich with his life story, and all the more helpful as each chapter offers key reflections on crucial developmental and formational topics. You will find yourself somewhere in this book and have a road map for what is ahead. Here is a book worthy of deeper reflection.'
Scott E. Shaum, director of pastoral advancement, Barnabas International

'*Footsteps of Faith* is more than Tony's wonderfully full and authentic life story – it holds deep and rich wisdom from someone living a life abandoned to the glory of God. There is much insight here for anyone navigating life and particularly those in church leadership. The book is well informed and provides opportunity to reflect on one's own season of life. I wholeheartedly recommend *Footsteps of Faith*.'
Morne Smit, pastor, God First Church, Christchurch

'This is a wonderful book for every stage of life, whether reflectively looking back, managing the present, or preparing for the future. It's backed by solid research but reads easily, good narrative as well as specific points to slow down and consider, with a challenge to think carefully and respond healthily. It's heartwarming without ducking difficulties. The reality of God's faithfulness within the ups and down of the Christian life, working with churches and mission agencies, is helpfully considered. God wants to work in us for change and through us for fruitfulness. We learn about "falling into grace", and becoming more than doing. This is a book to read and benefit from, then to pass on to others.'
Alan Tower, Friends International National director (UK)

 Ministries

15 The Chambers, Vineyard
Abingdon OX14 3FE
+44(0)1865 319700 | brf.org.uk

Bible Reading Fellowship (BRF) is a charity (233280) and company limited by guarantee (301324), registered in England and Wales

EU Authorised Representative: Easy Access System Europe – Mustamäe tee 50, 10621 Tallinn, Estonia, **gpsr.requests@easproject.com**

ISBN 978 1 80039 439 1
First published 2026
10 9 8 7 6 5 4 3 2 1 0

A catalogue record for this book is available from the British Library

Printed and bound by CPI Group (UK) Ltd, Croydon CR0 4YY

TONY HORSFALL

FOOTSTEPS OF FAITH

*Reflections from a lifetime
of following Jesus*

BRF
Ministries

CONTENTS

O let me see thy footsteps,
And in them plant mine own;
My hope to follow duly
Is in thy strength alone.
O guide me, call me, draw me,
Uphold me to the end;
And then in heaven receive me,
My Saviour and my friend.

John Ernest Bode (1816–74)

ACKNOWLEDGEMENTS

Many people have been part of the rich tapestry of my life, but it has not been possible to acknowledge here the contribution that each has made to my growth and development. You are nonetheless special, and your names are written on my heart. I will always treasure your friendship and wisdom and your place in my story. Know that, as the apostle Paul would have said, 'I thank my God every time I remember you.'

I am grateful to my wife Jilly for patiently reading through the manuscript chapter by chapter, making helpful comments, and asking pertinent questions. Still in the early days of our marriage, this discipline provided us with a crash course in 'getting to know you.' You are aware I am no super-saint, but happily you still love me! You are a wonderful companion.

Thanks also to others who read the first drafts and helped shape both the contents and tone of the material.

I am so proud of my children Alistair and Debbie, and their amazing families. You shared much of this journey with your lovely Mum and I, both the joys and the sorrows. You are deeply loved and much appreciated.

Finally, huge thanks to my publishers, BRF Ministries, for believing in me as a writer for more than 20 years and now giving me the opportunity to share my story.

FOREWORD

It was the American evangelist D.L. Moody who reputedly summarised the life of Moses with the observation that he 'spent forty years thinking he was somebody, forty years learning he was nobody, and forty years discovering what God can do with a nobody.' It's folksy wisdom, for sure, but in its simplicity it draws our attention to the developmental work that takes place across a leader's spiritual journey.

In his first letter, the apostle John writes about 'children', 'young men' and 'fathers'. A good case can be made for the idea that he is describing three stages of spiritual development. The children are new believers who are rejoicing that their sins are forgiven and that they have a heavenly Father. Further along, the young men are strong and engaged in spiritual conflict. And then there are the fathers: those who – in the words of John Stott – 'possess the depth and stability of ripe Christian experience.'[1] It's a compelling vision of the spiritual journey.

It may not feel to us that our journeys fall into such neat chronological classification, but it is helpful, not least as we get further along, to trace the ways that God has been at work in leading us. As Kierkegaard reminded us, while life has to be lived forwards, it is best understood backwards; or, in the words of William Bridges with which this book begins, 'it is only in seeing where you have been that you can tell where you are headed.'

The book you are about to embark on is Tony Horsfall's look back at where he has been and how God has led him to where he is today. Some of you will already have come across some of Tony's story or encountered his teaching on one of his retreats, or in one of the considerable number of books he has written previously. You will recognise the wise and gentle voice of a man who has walked with God through several decades and through several seasons.

It is a beautiful story, told with a humble and unassuming candour that doesn't rush past the jagged edges of disappointment or the reality of pain, yet points us unmistakably to the gracious guiding hand of a loving Father.

Part of the genius of the book is the way Tony has not merely recounted a sequential collection of stories from his life, but he has carefully drawn from each of the episodes key learning that has formed his path of discipleship. This in turn allows him to gently prompt us towards reflection with a set of wise and probing questions designed to help us to review our own adventure in following Jesus.

You will find this book to be a delight, and it will enrich you whatever your stage of life.

Dr Alan Wilson
Bible college tutor, author of The Crucible of Leadership and host of The Leadership Journey Podcast.

INTRODUCTION

You, an autobiographer? Why you? Why now? Because it is only in seeing where you have been that you can tell where you are headed.
William Bridges[2]

There comes a moment in life when we look back and ask ourselves, 'What was my life all about? What did it amount to?'

We may reach that place with a feeling of sadness and regret, wishing things had been different. More hopefully, we may come to the point of evaluation with a sense of satisfaction and fulfilment, feeling we have accomplished something meaningful during our brief time on planet earth.

As I look back over my own life, I am fortunate to feel more satisfaction than regret. Indeed, now in my 76th year, gratitude would be my overall emotion. I have so much to be thankful for despite my mistakes and shortcomings, and the painful episodes I have been through. For this I am truly gratefull to God.

My ambition, from my youth, has been to follow God's will for my life. I have aspired to live as well as I can as a disciple of Jesus and to walk in his footsteps. The way has not always been easy and there has been some rough terrain and moments of danger, but at the same time there has always been much joy along the way. Many times, God's presence has been undeniably real and his blessing unforgettably tangible. It has been, and continues to be, a great adventure.

At a conference some years ago, a lady asked about my life. Having mentioned a few highlights, she said to me, 'My, you have had an interesting life!' I guess I have, but what disturbed me was her use of the past tense, as if it were almost over! It is not! I am still going strong and still enjoying the adventure of faith – present tense!

It has been said that to be a person is to have a story to tell. My aim in this book is to share with you some of my story (which I hope you will find interesting) and to highlight some lessons from my life of discipleship which may be helpful to you in reflecting on your own spiritual journey. This is not, therefore, an autobiography in the strictest sense of the word. I am not writing so much about what I have done as about what God has done in me and through me. I am not recounting my accomplishments but describing God's dealings with me down the years. From this perspective, it could perhaps be called a *spiritual* autobiography, where the story is being written by God. He is, after all, the author and finisher of our faith (Hebrews 12:2, KJV), and we are simply caught up into his bigger story.

In reflecting on my life, I have found it helpful to have in mind a framework or road map for understanding how God typically works in his servants over the years. I have been helped in my thinking by *The Making of a Leader* by Dr J. Robert Clinton, a book which aims to provide biblical insights into the patterns and processes God uses to develop leaders over their lifetime. His ideas are the fruit of studying the lives of hundreds of biblical, historical, and contemporary figures. He writes, 'Effective spiritual ministry flows out of our being, and God is concerned with our being. He is forming it. The patterns and processes he uses to shape us are worthwhile subjects for leadership study.'[3] Clinton's work, although perhaps too mechanical and prescriptive, has helped many to understand some of the ways by which God is likely to be at work in us, and to recognise the contours of the spiritual journey.

A second significant work has been *The Critical Journey* by Janet Hagberg and Robert Guelich.[4] They focus more on identifying the stages of faith, the seasons of life we go through on the journey of discipleship. Everyone's journey is unique, but there are enough significant similarities to discern certain stages that we will pass through as we follow Jesus over a lifetime. Their material certainly rings true with me and with others with whom I have shared it. Again, it has given me a lens for understanding and a way of describing my own spiritual journey.

A summary of both approaches is found in the Appendix section. These may be helpful to refer to as you follow my story.

Although I am writing with leaders in mind, I am not thinking solely about them. I hope that what I share is equally applicable to anyone who seeks to live for God, whatever their calling or stage of life.

Of course, this is by necessity an edited version of my story, limited by my purpose and by the word count of a book of this size. Like the gospel writers, I have been selective in what I have included and have not attempted to recall every incident in my life (how tedious), even some of the important ones. No doubt afterwards my mind will be full of thoughts I could have shared, but I must draw the line somewhere. It is limited, too, by the vagaries of my memory, which is fading fast, so I have written now while I can still recall most things! In matters of controversy and conflict, I can only give my own perspective, which others may see differently, but I have sought to be honest and fair throughout and always respectful of others. Any errors of fact are my own responsibility.

When asked, 'What does your father do?' my daughter was at a loss for words to describe the nature of my work. She came up with the expression, 'Well, he's a kind of religious Indiana Jones!' I like that, although it may be a slight exaggeration. It does capture, though, the adventure of following Jesus – often exciting, sometimes daunting, occasionally scary, but always worthwhile and certainly never boring.

It may be helpful to explain the structure of the book, and how you may use it. Each chapter reflects a specific period of my life and begins with a narrative section telling my story. Added to that is a more general reflection about an aspect of how God may be at work in our lives during that stage. Finally, there are some questions for reflection (a point of connection with you, the reader) so that if you wish, you can ponder your own journey with God, and even, if it seems appropriate, to work on a personal timeline.

Some readers will be happy simply to enjoy the narrative by itself. Others will appreciate also the reflections to help them understand more about how God typically works within us on our journey with him. A few will use the questions as well, taking the opportunity to look at their own story, reflecting on the past and anticipating the future. Use the book in the way which most appeals to you.

Whatever approach you take, my prayer is that, as you read, you too may be inspired to follow Jesus wherever he leads you; and that as you read you will find yourself offering your life to God again in a joyful surrender to his amazing love.

1

BEGINNING

'Before I formed you in the womb I knew you, before you were born I set you apart; I appointed you as a prophet to the nations.'
JEREMIAH 1:5

Much of God's early preparation in our lives goes on below the surface, so to speak, and the ultimate results are often not apparent until much later... God's formation of our lives is mostly invisible to us at first.
Randy Reese and Robert Loane[5]

It's a cold, blustery day in March 1950. In the small mining village of Brierley in Yorkshire, in the north of England, two brothers are outside playing – Dave (14) and Sam (12).

A lady passes by and says casually, 'Hey, your mother's just had a baby.'

'She has not,' they say indignantly.

'She has,' says the lady, 'and it's a boy.'

Startled by this unexpected news, the brothers run home as fast as they can and burst into the house. They are shocked to see their mother holding a newborn baby. Dave, overwhelmed by this unexpected development, runs upstairs and refuses to come down. Sam disappears outside again, saying nothing.

Next morning when the two of them come down for breakfast, mother greets them with the baby, a little boy. 'Well then, what do you think?' she asks. 'Shall we keep him?'

There is a pause. 'I suppose so,' says Dave, resignedly.

Such was my entrance into the world and arrival into my family. Not the most auspicious beginning! I was a surprise, but not unwanted. I was the youngest of five children, Dave being the eldest, then Sam, and then my sisters, Dorothy (8) and Jean (5). The age of my parents, and the gap between myself and the others, suggest I may not have been a planned addition, but I was anticipated by God and not an accident or mistake. Another mouth to feed when times in post-war Britain were hard, but welcomed, nonetheless.

Made for a purpose

I find much comfort from the word of God to the young prophet, Jeremiah. Whatever the circumstances of his birth, his arrival into the world was carefully planned by God, and he was known to God even before he was formed in the womb. He was designed by God for a specific calling, to be a prophet to the nations, and his life unfolded in the light of this. His personality, gifting, and life experience all prepared him for his God-given assignment.

The same is true of each of us. We are created for a purpose. There are no 'accidents' with God, and we enter the world known and loved by our creator and maker. Hopefully this basic belovedness is communicated and confirmed to us by our parents and carers, but since there are no perfect parents and many damaged ones, most of us find it hard to believe that we are loved without condition. We spend much of our lives searching for connection, with God and others.

Childhood influences

Attachment science (or theory) is the study of how we make and keep connection with others, including God. Our style of relating is formed in the first months of life. If we experience closeness and feel safe and loved, we learn to trust and build relationships easily. If we experience separation and feel unsafe and unloved, then we may be insecure in relationships and anxious and fearful in life. Each of us develops our own unique and mostly unconscious attachment style, which affects how we relate both to other people and to God.

Although much of this happens before we are able to hold memories, reflecting on what we know of our early years can help us form some idea of our childhood experiences and help us identify how the presence or absence of love and connection has shaped us. Krispin Mayfield writes, 'Attachment styles are the profiles of our basic approach to relationships. They are the patterns of how we seek and maintain closeness and connection, and they tend to be consistent over the course of our lives. It's an aspect of our personality that imparts how we relate to parents, spouses, children, God, and anyone who is important to us.'[6]

So how did this work out for me?

We lived in a semi-detached council-owned house on a newish estate of similar houses, the house heated by a coal fire which belched black smoke into the atmosphere, as did all the others. Life was simple and basic. My father worked at the local coal mine, hard manual work, and very dangerous. Money was in short supply, wages being low. Dad had an allotment where he grew vegetables and flowers. His own child-hood had been difficult, and he rarely spoke about it. He smoked and went to the pub but never got drunk. I would describe him as being a good man, but distant. He didn't get angry and was never unkind or violent. He seldom raised his voice, but he rarely praised us. He did not want us to become proud or big-headed, characteristics unappreci-ated in a close-knit working-class culture.

Later in my life I came to realise that when I thought of God as my Father, I regarded him as good but remote and unlikely to say good things to me, that is, until I died – and then I might receive a 'Well done, good and faithful servant.' In the meantime, it was a case of working hard, hoping I was doing alright and that he was pleased with me. Like many believers, I had a lot to learn about the true Father heart of God with his unconditional love and approval, and his many ways of affirming his children.

Mum was the one we would turn to for comfort, and I felt I could tell her anything. She didn't have a paid job but looked after the family. An abiding image is of her sitting by the fireside, pen and notebook in hand, trying to make ends meet on Dad's poor wages. We often owed money to the local store and bought groceries 'on tick'. I went to school with my socks darned and holes in my shoes. She knitted, and we wore jumpers she had made. We learned to value what we had and to be careful with money. Her kindness made me feel safe, and home was a happy place. This meant my image of God was not totally defective. I had an instinctive awareness that there was a God and felt he too would be kind and good, if a little distant.

Family factors

At some point in my preschool years, I spent a short time in an isolation hospital, although I'm not sure why. I have a memory of being in a cot with high metal sides. I'm told that when I came home, I was ravenous and would eat anything, especially crusts of bread. This separation must have been traumatic for a young boy used to being part of a big family. I often think this may be one of the reasons why I never used to enjoy being alone. I had an unconscious fear of abandonment which has been there throughout my life.

Because Dave and Sam were so much older than me, I never really felt I had brothers. I didn't see much of them, and they were more like uncles to me. I was closer to my sisters, Jean in particular, although she too was a fair bit older than me. There were plenty of other children to play with on the estate, and street games were popular, but I often played by myself as well. I loved roaming the fields and hedgerows, looking for birds nests and identifying them by their eggs. Perhaps even then my tendency towards introversion was forming.

Recognition of God

Ours was not a family with faith. There was no Bible in the home, and I never remember anyone ever praying with me. We didn't go to church as a whole family and God was never mentioned. What we knew about God came from school and from being sent to Sunday school at the village chapel.

I attended the village primary school which was connected to the Church of England. It meant that we were taught Bible stories and would go to the nearby church for Christmas, Easter, and Harvest festival. The pipe-smoking vicar would lead the services and tell us stories but made no attempt to help us find personal faith. I loved school and was keen to learn. The headmaster, Mr Balmforth, was my hero and I think his example made me want to become a teacher myself. Even then I can see leadership traits developing in me. I managed to pass my eleven-plus exams, gaining me entrance to the nearby grammar school which opened the door further to the love of learning, enjoyment of all kinds of sports, and becoming a leader.

In the 1950s it was still popular to go to either church or chapel, and we definitely identified as chapel people – which was considered more working-class – even though we didn't attend as a family. In many ways the Methodist chapel was at the heart of life in the village, and I joined my sisters in going regularly. Here we made friends with children our own age, did lots of fun things, but also learnt more about the Bible. Once a year, we would tour the village on tractors and trailers singing specially prepared songs to celebrate the Sunday school anniversary. Then we went back to chapel for cakes and tea, followed by games in a nearby field and ice creams. They were special days filled with simple pleasures! The first books I ever owned (mostly Enid Blyton) were prizes for attendance at the Sunday school and created in me a love of reading. My belief in God was strengthened by all of this, and while I was not yet converted, I was becoming more spiritually aware.

God's hidden work

Much of God's work in our lives in our earliest years is hidden from view, but reflecting on our past can help us to trace his hand in our lives from the moment of our birth (and even before). Dr J. Robert Clinton calls this phase 'sovereign foundations', when God is working providentially in our lives to bring us to himself and prepare us for the plan he has for our life. Our family or origin, the period of history we grew up in, the social culture into which we were born, and the things that happened to us, all shape who we become in later life. God weaves together all the bits and pieces of our lives into his unique design for us, even when we are not aware of it. God's formation of us in our earliest years is mostly invisible, beneath the surface, and often only becomes apparent later.

This was me, then, up to the age of eleven. I had safely navigated the childhood years without too much upset and was ready to enter my teenage years full of hope and confidence. I was aware of God and yet had no personal relationship with him, but he had made me for himself and was about to make himself known to me more fully. Then my life would really begin, but I could never have imagined the far-reaching plans God had for me, a working-class lad, hidden away in a tiny mining village in the north of England.

Reflection 1:

DESIGNED FOR A PURPOSE

Our childhood years provide the root system for our adult lives, often hidden from view but crucially important and continuing to influence who we are and how we live long after we have grown up. This is why it is helpful to reflect on our childhood and to understand how we have been formed and shaped by things that happened to us long ago.

God is at work in our lives before ever we come to know him, building foundations for the future. God has always been at work in our lives in ways that prepare us for his purpose. From Jeremiah 1:5 we learn that this work predated even our birth, God creating us with his purpose in mind, and placing within us certain gifts and personality traits that make us who we are. David wonderfully describes in amazing detail this creative act of God in Psalm 139:13–18, summed up in the expression that we have been 'fearfully and wonderfully made' (v. 14). He also connects the way we have been made with God's plan for our life, paraphrased in *The Message* like this: 'Like an open book, you watched me grow from conception to birth; all the stages of my life were spread out before you, the days of my life all prepared before I'd even lived one day' (v. 16).

With such a background, we can see that each of us has an intrinsic worth, value, and dignity. The apostle Paul concurs with this, saying, 'For we are God's handiwork, created in Christ Jesus to do good works, which God prepared in advance for us to do' (Ephesians 2:10). The word translated here as 'handiwork' is the Greek word *poiema* and means literally a work of art, a piece of craftsmanship. It is the word from which we get the word 'poem', an apt description of the creativity of God as he writes his message to the world through the story of our individual lives.

There is therefore a real sense in which we begin life with something of God's imprint on us, something which has been given to us and is there by grace, but other factors also shape us into the people we become, especially in our earlier years. Formative influences during childhood include the cultural and historical setting of our early years, our family background and history, the social milieu of our life, and the spiritual ethos (or lack of it) in which we grew up. That which is given is because of nature (or God), that which comes later is nurture; we are products of both.

Looking at my own story, I grew up in the 1950s, a period of optimism after the end of World War II, but still a time of austerity and simple living. I am therefore a 'baby boomer', one of the generation fortunate to be born in Britain after the war and into the welfare state with improving health care and better educational opportunities. I was a working-class boy, growing up in the industrial part of Yorkshire and absorbing the values of that context – hard working, thrifty with money, suspicious of privilege, and careful not to get above my station in life.

These were also the values of my family of origin, along with a guarding of our privacy, a dislike of too much emotion, a despising of showing off, an avoidance of conflict, and an aversion to asking for help. We were not physically expressive and seldom talked deeply of heart matters. Our horizons were limited and our exposure to people 'not like us' was infrequent. Spiritually, what we knew of God came from outside influences – a church school and the Methodist chapel. Religion was plain and simple, practical in expression and not at all showy. As you can see, much in my life needed changing and expanding!

Furthermore, since most of us are unaware of God in our early years, we inherit from our family and social network ways of behaving to get by in the world on our own. These habitual patterns become our default position and are deeply ingrained. We can describe them also as 'flesh patterns' since they have their origin in what the Bible calls the 'flesh' – the sinful, independent self that does not know God. They may be helpful or unhelpful, but either way they express the human tendency to try to manage life without God. At some point later in life these will be exposed as inadequate, even destructive, and we will need to learn new ways that reflect our growing dependency on God.

During this period, God's working in our lives may be invisible and it may be only when we take time to reflect that we can begin to see his hand at work shaping us and directing our path. For some this may be an easy and joyful thing to do as we discover that God has been lovingly present and active all along. For others it will be difficult because our early years were painful and traumatic and contain memories long since buried and hidden away. We may need skilled help to explore the darkness and confront the pain, but this will be necessary if we are to find healing and the freedom to become more fully the person God has made us to be.

Randy Reese and Robert Loane say that if we neglect to return to the beginning, there may well be fault lines which will appear later in our life and leadership. They write, 'We will come to learn that the leadership we provide essentially flows out of who we are. And if we have not come to honest terms with who we are, eventually that will show itself when the work of leadership becomes more stressful and challenging.'[7]

Our awareness that we have been designed for a purpose may not dawn upon us until we are much older, but it is still true in childhood. Latent within us are gifts, talents, and abilities which will hopefully blossom and flourish as we discover who God is, the purpose he has for our lives, and then give ourselves wholly in response, but this will take time. Through the ups and downs of life, even in childhood, our character is taking shape and our personality beginning to shine through. The great danger, though, is that we try to be something other than who God designed us to be, fearing that, somehow, in ourselves we are not enough.

How does this happen? Other people may not like us as we are and may pressurise us to conform to their expectations for us. Life may squeeze us into its own mould, inviting us to do what is popular, profitable, necessary, and acceptable. Our own self-doubt may push us into paths that lead us away from who we really are and into more comfortable choices. The pain and trauma we experience may require us to adopt a different persona simply to survive. Thus, we may lose touch with our original self, and the purpose of God, and develop a false self (not in the sense of being evil, but simply not authentic), wearing it like a set of clothes to cover who we really are. In this way the spiritual journey becomes a search for one's true self, and it may take many years to discover that we are not really being who we were created to be, and then to have the courage to search for the lost part of us.

Psychologist and spiritual director Dr David Benner says, 'Being most deeply your unique self is something that God desires, because your true self is grounded in Christ. God created you in uniqueness and seeks to restore you to that uniqueness in Christ. Finding and living out your true self is fulfilling your destiny.'[8]

The spiritual life is therefore a journey into the discovery of who we truly are, and the purpose for which we were actually made – in other words, our vocation. This is a journey that begins when we first come to Christ and hear his call to discipleship, a call not just to follow him, but to be with him and become like him.

Point of connection

Allow my story and the following reflection to stimulate your own thinking about your early childhood. Let the thoughts come freely, along with any emotions. This may require that you set time aside where you can think reflectively, with the help of God's Spirit.

- Can you see how God has been at work in your early years, building his sovereign foundations?

- How may you have been shaped by your family of origin, the society in which you grew up, your geographical location at the time, and the culture of the day?

- As you look back over your earliest years, do you feel you have any attachment issues? Has there been significant trauma which has not been attended to?

- What gifts, talents, and abilities do you think have been there since birth, part of the way God made you with his purpose in mind? Why not give thanks for this?

You may like to make a timeline of your life, dividing it into the different decades. Then add significant moments and places to illustrate your journey. You might put positive experiences above the line, negative ones beneath the line. Use colours if that helps to identify key thoughts. This will take some time and thought, and there is no rush to do it, but it could be a helpful exercise alongside reading the book.

2

FOLLOWING

But God demonstrates his own love for us in this: while we were still sinners, Christ died for us.

ROMANS 5:8

If I see my life as story, I know it to be an invitation to enter the great adventure, battle, and drama of the unfolding narrative of my life in a world that is inhabited with the presence and voice of God.

Keith Anderson[9]

I remember my first day at Hemsworth Grammar School very clearly. All the first-year pupils (aged eleven), drawn from the surrounding villages and proudly wearing their new school uniforms, were ushered into the dining room for an assembly. I was in the centre of the front row, right under the gaze of Mr Collett, the deputy head, stern-faced and intimidatingly dressed in a black academic gown, worn over his normal clothes.

He placed his notes down on the table in front of me and stepped back as he waited for everyone to take their places. Innocently I peered forward to see if I could read what he had written, but he saw me.

'Do you normally read other people's correspondence?' he bellowed in a voice the like of which I had never heard before. I was shaken to the core of my being and totally humiliated.

'No, sir,' I responded shakily.

'Then don't try to read mine,' he said firmly, before beginning his address to the assembled students.

Secondary school

I never did like Mr Collett after that, but fortunately he never taught me, and I gave him a wide berth. Discipline was strong at the school, and offenders were caned. A stripes and stars board publicly showed those whose work was good and shamed those whose work and behaviour were not up to scratch. Sixth-form pupils served as prefects and enforced school rules, often with a heavy hand. For some reason, a favourite penalty imposed on miscreants was to make them write out Psalm 119. I am not sure if this religious exercise enabled or hindered their rehabilitation, or their love of God! One friend who was unjustly picked on by the prefects left the school in the second year because he could take no more bullying.

Once I understood how things worked in this new environment, I was fine and thrived in a school that valued academic achievement and sporting excellence. The grammar school system had its detractors, but it was a gateway for many of us working-class children to aspire to higher things. I particularly liked to read the honours board in the school hall, where the names of those who had gone on to graduate from university were celebrated in gold lettering. I thought, 'One day, that will be me.'

The playing fields were broad and expansive, with rugby and hockey pitches, tennis courts, and, given pride of place, the cricket square. I remember the excitement I felt when I was selected for the first rugby match with the under-twelves, an away game at a school in York. Then, in the summer, learning how to play cricket and realising I could both bat and bowl. The same ambition that fired my academic dreams fuelled my sporting hopes – one day to play for the First XV at rugby and the First XI at cricket.

Intertwined with studies and sport, the school provided other opportunities for growth and development. Chess club and choir were popular, but I enjoyed drama and took part in several school plays. I was never a good actor but doing things publicly on stage helped develop my self-confidence.

Teenage years and faith

Life was full in my teenage years, and I was still loosely attached to the chapel. Without realising it, I was growing in spiritual awareness. My sister Jean asked me if I would like to go with her to hear some students from Cliff College, a Methodist training establishment in Derbyshire. They were holding special meetings at the chapel, and she thought I would enjoy it as a lot of the young people were going along.

I remember it was an August evening, and I was 14. I went with no expectations at all but was gripped by what the young preacher had to say. For the first time, as far as I can remember, I heard a gospel message – that we were all sinners, and that Christ had died so we might be forgiven and come back into a relationship with God. It affected me deeply, so much so that when he invited anyone who wanted to respond to go out to the altar rail at the front of the church, I was the first to go. I moved forward with tears rolling down my cheeks.

Growing as a disciple

The seed of new life was sown in my heart that night, and although I didn't realise it at the time, the course of my life had been set – I had become a follower of Jesus. Two people came into my life at this point and both helped me to grow in my discipleship. Now we would say they 'mentored' me, but neither used the term. They simply wanted to help me grow as a Christian, and I entered the period that Janet Hagberg and Robert Guelich call 'the life of discipleship'.

The first was Dennis Bavister, a young teacher newly arrived at the grammar school and a keen Christian. He came to live in Brierley and started to attend the chapel. At school he taught R.E. and made it interesting and accessible for us, sharing with us stories like the conversion of New York gang member Nicky Cruz in *The Cross and the Switchblade*. Keen on the outdoors, he led several groups from school on trips to Wales where we hiked in the mountains. When he invited some of us to his home on Saturday evenings for Bible study (it was a different time back then, and I'm aware this wouldn't and shouldn't happen today), I was excited to attend. We formed a Christian group in the school, and there was a real move of God, with several of us eventually finding our way into full-time ministry. Dennis gave me a love for the scriptures and emphasised the cost of discipleship. I learnt that to follow Jesus is to give your life completely to him.

The second was Eddie Hambleton who ran the youth club based at the chapel on Friday evenings, where we played table tennis, snooker, card games, and listened to pop music. Eddie was great fun and also strong in his faith. He invited me in the summer of 1966 to join him at a Christian Endeavour Holiday Centre on the south coast of England, working together as excursion leaders – organising a games programme for the guests, leading trips out to local tourist attractions, and taking occasional devotional times. It was very daunting at first – at 16 I was relatively shy, but gradually I came out of my shell and warmed to the job. We did similar stints the following two summers, in different holiday places, and developed a great friendship and rapport. Eddie introduced me to the adult world, showed confidence in me, and helped my gift of leadership to come to the surface.

A call to serve?

It was during one of these summer work experiences that I began to sense God might be calling me to serve him. What I had in mind was to train as a teacher and then perhaps become a local church pastor. When I shared this with Dennis, he suggested I consider applying to London Bible College, where he himself had trained. The prospectus looked interesting, and the staff were all highly qualified. They offered a degree from London University and were keen to broaden their scope from a narrow focus on ministerial formation to training for Christian service in general. I went for interview, and although only 18 at the time, was accepted for the Bachelor of Divinity course.

My parents were a little uncertain about all this at first, fearing I might be throwing away the opportunity of a good education and career, but they could see it was what I wanted to do and gave me their blessing. To everyone's surprise, I was given a university grant for three years from the local education authority, and that seemed to be a good indication that, even though I was quite young, this was indeed the right path for me. I was still quite naïve in my faith, not well grounded in doctrine, and not very experienced in church matters, but my heart was set in the right direction.

While preparing for my A-level exams and waiting to go to college, opportunities came to take part in leading church services. The local Methodist churches had a mission band, a group of young people coached by an experienced lay preacher, and I joined them. We were far from polished, but it was good experience. I shudder now to think of some of the things I said in my first attempts at preaching! One issue loomed large in my life, however, which I knew I needed to sort out. I was going out with a girl at the time, and our relationship was veering in the wrong direction. I saw too that we did not have the same vision for the future, and so reluctantly we parted ways. It was the first time I had to say to God, 'Not my will but yours be done,' and it was painful for us both. A little act of costly obedience, and a crucial moment in my discipleship journey.

Never too young

I am encouraged that when Jeremiah wanted to opt out of God's call because of his inexperience, God said to him, 'Do not say, "I am too young"' (Jeremiah 1:7). Paul also said to Timothy, 'Don't let anyone look down on you because you are young' (1 Timothy 4:12). Mary, the mother of Jesus, was just a teenage girl when she said her 'Yes' to God's call (Luke 1:38). Others recognised God's hand on my life despite my youthfulness and opened the door to a period of preparation for life and ministry. I am so grateful for these people who helped me to grow as a disciple and shaped my early years as a follower of Jesus.

Randy Reese and Robert Loane in their book *Deep Mentoring* make this observation: 'One of the common denominators apparent in those who lived well, led well, and finished well was that they had people – mentors, teachers, advisers, counsellors, guides, friends – who had the love, patience, and courage to walk alongside them and through various seasons along the journey.'[10] This was certainly my experience, and perhaps it is the reason why I have given so much of my time over the years to mentoring others.

Reflection 2:

THE ESSENCE OF DISCIPLESHIP

One of the major weaknesses of the western church is that we have many church attenders, but not so many disciples. With a background of cultural Christianity, many are happy to take the name 'Christian' but never realise the implications of what it truly means. They are happy to attend church occasionally, but have never either heard, or responded to, the claims of Jesus upon their lives. Consequently, a form of non-discipleship Christianity is prevalent in many churches, which greatly reduces the effectiveness of their mission in the world as well as robbing individuals of the joy of a full-blown relationship with Jesus.

From my earliest days as a believer, I was taught that the call to follow Jesus is to be taken seriously. As Bill Hull says, 'Discipleship isn't a programme or an event; it's a way of life. It's not for a limited time, but for a whole life.'[11] Encouraged to read the Bible regularly, I saw for myself that Jesus called his followers to give themselves fully to him and his purpose in the world. When he called those first fishermen-disciples, they left their nets and followed him gladly. He taught them this principle: 'Whoever wants to be my disciple must deny themselves and take up their cross and follow me. For whoever wants to save their life will lose it, but whoever loses their life for me and for the gospel will save it' (Mark 8:34–35). Clearly, there is a cost to following Jesus, but surrendering to his will for our lives is the way in which we discover purpose, meaning, and fulfilment.

Such a surrender does not come easily, however, and for me, as for most would-be disciples, there was a battle to be fought – between what we want and what God wants. It is relatively easy to come to know Jesus as Saviour, with the attendant benefits of forgiveness and new life, but an altogether different matter to crown him as Lord of our lives. There will often be a specific battle ground where the issue of control is fought out. In my own case it involved yielding my involvement in sport to God and, as I have already mentioned, relinquishing a relationship that was unhelpful. I was good at sport, but increasingly games were played on Sundays, and we were taught that church attendance should have the priority. Nowadays Christians have a more open attitude to Sunday sport, seeing the opportunity to be involved with those without faith as a natural way to build relationships. In the 1960s this was not the case, and sadly my sport had to take a back seat.

Both decisions were painful, but both opened my heart more fully to God and prepared me for embracing his good and perfect will for my life. Both were testing grounds, helping me to learn obedience and submission to God. What made this possible for me was the knowledge of a greater love, Jesus' love for me, displayed so magnificently at the cross. In the words of a great hymn, 'Love so amazing, so divine, Demands my soul, my life, my all' (Isaac Watts, 1674–1748). This was my motivation.

These early decisions established in my heart what we might call the 'God-first' principle, on which all our following of Jesus rests. It is summed up in Matthew 6:33 where we read, 'Seek first his kingdom and his righteousness, and all these things will be given to you as well.' Jesus is King, and his kingdom is established in the hearts of those who allow him to rule in their lives. Discipleship is about kingdom living and bringing every aspect of our lives under his control, but it is a kingdom of love where we are invited to offer ourselves willingly to God, but never under compulsion.

Two questions emerge for many young people who take discipleship seriously – the question of career (what will I do with my life?) and that of marriage (whom will I marry, if I am to marry at all?). These would both be worked out for me in the next phase of my life, but already in my decision to apply to London Bible College I was responding to what I felt was a call to ministry and offering myself to God for whatever he had in mind for me.

Not all are called to full-time ministry, however, and for most the call of God will lead them into a normal career path where they can serve God as wholeheartedly as anyone in ministry. Neither path is more valid than the other. The important thing is that we make ourselves available to God and seek, with the help of others, to discern his direction for our lives, responding with faith and obedience to whatever he says.

As I have gone through life seeking to follow Jesus, other 'crossroads' moments have occurred where once again the choice would be between doing my own will or that of God. In some ways, when we have experienced the blessing that comes from obedience and surrender, every new point of decision becomes a little easier since we know that God's will is ultimately the best and for our good, yet because we are human, we may still find it difficult to yield ourselves again. One thing that has helped me enormously in recent years is the awareness that, in the words of David Benner, surrender to God is always surrender to love – not to power, control, or authority.[12]

Benner notes that a focus on obedience in isolation from love can result in a begrudging compliance rather than a glad offering of oneself in love to the prior love of God. Our difficulties in obedience are not a matter of the will, but of the heart, of not realising how deeply we are loved or how much God desires our deepest happiness. If we are not convinced of God's good intention, we are unlikely to yield the control of our lives to him. Benner suggests that saying 'Yes' to God 'begins as I experience his wildly enthusiastic, recklessly loving affirmation of me. It grows out of soaking myself in this love so thoroughly that love for God springs up in response. Surrender to his love is the work of the Spirit, making his love ours and his nature ours.'[13]

What this means is that we can take no credit for our discipleship. We are simply responding to the love of God drawing us and wooing us into the path of life God has for us, the way of righteousness. Without the experience of God's love, however, discipleship may seem hard and difficult and may be forced upon us by overzealous leaders who demand our commitment. By contrast, when we are aware of the call of love our response can be one of glad abandonment to a life of exciting adventure lived in partnership with the one who loved us and gave himself for us.

Point of connection

Many people become followers of Jesus during their teenage years, as I did. If that was true for you, it may be helpful to reflect on the early foundations of your Christian life. Even if you became a believer later, it may still be helpful to reflect on your teenage years, and to consider the foundations of your faith.

- How would you describe your teenage years? How were the school years for you?

- When did you first respond to the invitation of Jesus to receive the gift of salvation, and become his disciple? How did that come about? What was it that drew you to Christ?

- Do you think you were well discipled, or was your growth in God taken for granted? How did this affect your spiritual progress, for better or worse?

- Did anyone play a significant part in your early discipleship journey? How did they help you? Do they know that you appreciated them?

- What were the early testing points that established the lordship of Christ in your life? How else were you working out the call to wholehearted discipleship – for example, in the choices you made on leaving school, or in forming relationships? How did your faith impact your decision-making?

- Did you have opportunities to learn more about your faith, serve other people, and develop any leadership potential during this period?

Continue to work on your timeline, doing more detailed work now on the first two decades. Why not talk to those who knew you during this period? What would they have to say about you?

3

TRAINING

Do your best to present yourself to God as one approved, a worker who does not need to be ashamed and who correctly handles the word of truth.

2 TIMOTHY 2:15

At this stage, we clearly are the learners, not the teachers. This is a taking stage, a filling stage. It feels very much like a one-way street. This means vulnerability, and some feelings of fear and even inadequacy accompany the excitement of new learning.

Janet Hagberg and Robert Guelich[14]

Moving down to live in London in 1968 from a small mining village in the north of England was a big step for me since I had travelled very little at this point. It was all a bit overwhelming, and I was grateful for another first-year student who showed me how to get around on the London Underground (The Tube). But settling in was not easy and during the first term I felt homesick and a bit lonely.

College life

London Bible College (LBC) was a hotbed of Calvinism and reformed theology, although I had no idea who Calvin was! I shared a room with two other lads, second years, and they found it hard to believe that a

Methodist could also be a true Christian. They sat me down on a chair, and with a few other students from our landing, went through the five points of Calvinism with me. I scored three out of five and passed the interrogation (just), but I realised I had a lot to learn. I must have gained their respect over time, though, because at the end of that year I was best man for one of them.

Those of us doing an external Bachelor of Divinity course from London University also had to study London Bible College subjects based around Bible books and the practicalities of ministry, so we worked hard. We had classes in the morning, free afternoons, then study periods each evening. At weekends we were allocated to church-based teams and Sunday was spent at our placement, which in my first two years was at The Strangers' Rest Mission in the East End of London. Each day we had college chapel, and on Wednesdays a visiting speaker. There was much to learn and take in as I entered the world of evangelicalism.

Gradually I settled down, made good friendships, and threw myself into college life. As at school, my ability in sport meant I was involved in many teams and made friends easily. I loved the interaction with the overseas students I met. Several came home with me during the holidays and hosting people from Africa was a huge eye-opener for my parents, but they made them all feel welcome. I guess these friendships were formative in giving me a world vision and broadening my horizons, which would be so significant in days to come. Maybe there was something latent inside me which was finding expression.

There were many opportunities for us to identify and use our giftings, as well as to grow in our ability to lead. I was involved in summer outreach teams, including leading one in Liverpool. We went out preaching regularly to churches in the London area and took the opportunity to visit some of the well-known churches in London to hear famous preachers like Dr Martyn Lloyd-Jones and John Stott. Their teaching impacted me, and I have loved expository preaching ever since.

Encountering the Spirit

In 1970 the college moved from central London to Northwood in the suburbs. The new campus was spacious and green, and a contrast to the cramped and dated accommodation we had in Marylebone Road. Somehow the whole feel of the college changed and it became more relaxed. Doctrinal disputes lessened and there was a more worshipful atmosphere. Perhaps this was my imagination, but I think not. The change coincided with the charismatic renewal movement that was sweeping the country at the time, and many students had been helpfully impacted. I recognised that they had a deeper level to their experience of God than I had, and I began to hunger to know more of the Holy Spirit's work in my life.

During one of the term breaks I went home to Yorkshire and one Sunday attended the village chapel. A young man was preaching about the Holy Spirit, and in summary said, 'The Spirit was given when Jesus was glorified, and he will be given to you when Jesus is glorified in your life'. I went home, straight upstairs to my bedroom, and got down on my knees. As best as I could, I offered myself to God again, and as I did so waves of love swept over me. I knew I had been filled with the Spirit. This feeling of closeness to God continued for a few days. I felt a great desire to pray and be with Jesus, and when I read my Bible, it felt like a new book, filled with wonderful words that spoke straight into my heart. It was a major turning point for me, an empowering moment without which I would have been unprepared to serve God. It was also the beginning of a continuing relationship with the Holy Spirit on which the fruitfulness of my ministry has depended to this very day.

I also became convicted of the need to be baptised by immersion. As I became more familiar with the New Testament, I saw that the order of salvation seemed to be repent and then be baptised (Acts 2:38). I could not remember my child baptism, and it had no significance for me, so I asked to be baptised in the church where I was based at the weekends back at college – Chorleywood Baptist Church, in Hertfordshire. My parents were worried by this, thinking I had joined a cult, and came down to London to check me out. When they came to the service, they saw how real it was and left for home happy I was alright and moved by the whole experience.

Life partner

One of the most important decisions we ever make in life is the choice of a life partner, and I was asking God to give me the right person to marry. In my final year of college (I had extended my course to four years to give more time to study the Bible), I met a fellow student to whom I was irresistibly drawn. Evelyn was from Inverness in Scotland and had been a nurse before feeling called to study at LBC, prior to going overseas. A couple of coincidences caused our paths to cross. She was sharing a room with a girl from my hometown of Barnsley whom I knew already, and we were both allocated to Chorleywood Baptist for our church assignment. I found I could talk to her easily, and I loved the way she cared for people in simple, thoughtful ways. I felt she would make a good pastor's wife, and of course, I found her very attractive.

We exchanged letters over the Christmas holidays and found we had both been given the same verses from God as we offered our futures to him - Ecclesiastes 4:9-10 which says, 'Two are better than one, because they have a good return for their labour; if either of them falls down, one can help the other up. But pity anyone who falls and has no one to help them up.' This coincidence seemed a confirmation to proceed with our friendship, which we did when the new term began.

Our relationship developed easily, but one obstacle stood in our way - Evelyn was feeling called to be a missionary nurse, while I was thinking of becoming a teacher and then doing pastoral work in this country. How would the dilemma be resolved? I felt sure that God would change Evelyn's mind, but it was me he spoke to about new possibilities.

A year earlier I had picked up a copy of the two-volume work on the life of Hudson Taylor (1832–1905), the great missionary to China. What I didn't know was that he came from Barnsley, my hometown! Furthermore, the first page of volume one begins with this sentence: 'The sun had not yet risen over Brierley Common.' Well, Brierley was my home village. I immediately sensed a connection with this great man of faith and wanted to find out more about him. I was challenged and inspired by his wholehearted commitment to God, and my eyes were being opened to wider possibilities.

The call to mission

Soon after I had met Evelyn, I was reading a book called *The Chinese Church That Will Not Die*, an account of the miraculous survival of the church after the Communist takeover of China in 1949. Written by Mary Wang, it is a remarkable story of the persecuted church, but what caught my attention was her assertion that a quarter of the world's population are Chinese. That night as I slept, I felt God say to me, 'That is a quarter of the world for whom Christ died,' and I felt a burden for the Chinese people enter my heart. Next morning I awoke with the realisation that I had some rethinking to do and needed to be open to a change of direction. Me, a missionary?

We continued to ponder our future together and began talking with the Overseas Missionary Fellowship (OMF), the mission Evelyn was already in touch with, about future possibilities. I appreciated their openness and lack of pressure, and the advice to take our time and come back to them later. My plan after Bible college was to do a teacher training course and then get a job teaching. I applied to Carnegie College in Leeds and was accepted. Evelyn had another year to go at college, so it meant we would be apart but that would test the reality of our relationship and my calling to mission.

I enjoyed my time at London Bible College and valued learning how to handle the Bible well, how to think doctrinally, and the exposure it gave to the wider church. In particular, I appreciated learning New Testament Greek and the insights this provides when reading the gospels and epistles – something which is always part of my preaching preparation even now. For this I must thank Peggy Knight, the only female member of staff, but perhaps the best teacher in the faculty. I also appreciated the pastoral care and friendship of Arthur Cundall, our Old Testament lecturer, who although in his 40s joined us on the football field as well. I felt grounded in my faith, confident in handling the Scriptures correctly, and assured in my calling to ministry. If there was a weakness, it was that there was little emphasis on personal discipleship, which seemed to be taken for granted, and nothing about how to lead a church or manage people.

God at work

This period of training and preparation for ministry is considered by leadership development theorists as typically about getting to know God more deeply and bringing one's life into line with his (termed by Dr J. Robert Clinton as 'inner life growth'). The focus is on our relationship with God, and God is working primarily in us rather than through us. Matters of obedience provide tests of our surrender to God and the integrity of our faith. Each time we align our lives with God, we prepare ourselves for him to use us in the future.

Looking back, this was certainly what was happening in me, although I was not conscious of it at the time. All I knew was that I wanted to serve God. I was taking one step at a time without seeing the bigger picture, but the guiding hand of God was at work.

Reflection 3:

SELF-KNOWLEDGE

There is a clear consensus nowadays that character formation is essential to the development of any effective ministry. Our character is the foundation stone on which the rest of our story and service will rest, and we must pay careful attention to the kind of person we are becoming. Too many gifted leaders have made a shipwreck of their faith, and damaged their followers in the process, simply because they did not pay adequate attention to their character. When the pressure was on, the unseen fault lines were tragically exposed.

God is always at work in us, shaping and forming us, and often using the circumstances of life to smooth off our rough edges and make us pliable in his hands. Through trials and difficulties, he tests our integrity (will we refuse to compromise?), our obedience (will we do as he says?), our faith (will we trust him?), and our fidelity (will we remain steadfast?). He wants us to become 'instruments for special purposes, made holy, useful to the Master and prepared to do any good work' (2 Timothy 2:21). This is a life-long process, and I was very conscious that this process was already underway within me during my time at Bible college. It was not simply a question of obtaining academic qualifications but of getting to know God more deeply. And in the melting pot of college life (there were over 200 students, male and female, with a wide variety of church backgrounds, theological persuasions, and nationalities), there was plenty of opportunity to be smoothed by the sandpaper of human interactions.

We may be tempted to feel that because character formation is God's work, we can be passive, simply allowing him to work in us but playing no part in the process ourselves. This is not the case. We are told clearly to work out our own salvation with fear and trembling because God is at work in us (Philippians 2:12–13). We are to be actively seeking to develop a sound character, albeit with God's help.

Rather than be passive, we are called to grow in self-awareness, learning to reflect on our behaviours and impact on others, as well as in self-understanding, seeking to know ourselves and what makes us 'tick' more fully. This refers to our strengths, as well as our weaknesses. Psychologist David Benner writes, 'Deep knowing of God and deep knowing of self always develop interactively. The result is the authentic transformation of the self that is the core of Christian spirituality.'[15] This is referred to as dual knowledge – as we know God we get to know ourselves; as we know ourselves, we come to understand God as well. It is a way by which we can help with our own character development.

Self-awareness relates mostly to our relationships. How do other people experience us, and is this helpful or not? It is possible to have blind spots and not realise that, for example, we speak too much, dominate conversations, and never listen to others. Likewise, we may have a habit of tuning out of conversations, so we appear uninterested or aloof. We may not know, for instance, that our habit of being late and disorganised irritates others, and that we are perceived as being unreliable. Unless such behaviours are pointed out to us, they may well be reinforced over time, making change more difficult and developing into a character flaw which may undermine the work we do and our effectiveness.

Self-understanding relates chiefly to our reactions, responses, and why we do the things we do. How do we respond to other people? For example, are we judgemental, critically assessing others and forming opinions about them without even realising? Do we habitually compare ourselves to others unfavourably, feeling intimidated by their success and jealous of their popularity? How do we react to criticism, being treated unfairly, or being under authority? Have we learned to recognise the signals that we are overtired, have taken on too much, and need a break? If we understand ourselves, we can better manage ourselves through stressful times and with difficult people without behaving badly.

These two forms of self-knowledge (self-awareness and self-understanding) are vital factors in our journey to maturity. I was in my early 20s and still quite young, but already learning to think reflectively. The ability to examine our ways increases as we get older, of course, and plays an important part in our development.

How then can we grow in self-knowledge?

Whenever we read *scripture*, we can learn more about human nature, and therefore about ourselves. As well as the moral exhortations we are given, the stories of men and women in the Bible are laid bare before us so that we can learn from their examples, both good and bad. We see our own lives reflected in theirs, and if we read wisely, we will take note of their mistakes and avoid walking in a similar way. In this way we allow the Bible to become a mirror to our souls and are constantly being challenged by its light. Paul says that the failures of the people of Israel in the Old Testament now serve as a reminder to us of the danger of complacency. He writes, 'These things happened to them as examples and were written down as warnings for us' (1 Corinthians 10:11). If I am reading well then the stories of Abraham, Moses, David, and others will become integrated into my own thinking, reinforcing good principles and guiding me past unhelpful ones.

Self-reflection is another way by which we grow in self-awareness, especially when we do this with the help of the Holy Spirit. Each day it is worth taking time to think back over our day and ask the questions, 'Where was God in my day? Where did I do the right thing, and when did I do what was wrong?' As we listen to the voice of the Spirit, we can then receive any necessary forgiveness, take note of any learning points for the future, and celebrate progress being made. As part of becoming more reflective we can learn to listen to the voice of conscience, which although not a perfect guide, is often the voice of God to us. Keeping a clear and tender conscience will help us in our self-awareness. It is when our conscience has been dulled that we are likely to be clumsy and insensitive to our own wrongdoing or carelessness.

Friends and trusted advisors can help us enormously in knowing ourselves better, and if we are married, so can our spouse. Not only can they affirm what is good in us, they can also challenge lovingly that which may be amiss, and that which we do not realise about ourselves. If we have the humility and courage to open ourselves up to others, seeking their help and counsel, welcoming feedback and correction, our journey to maturity will be accelerated and we may well avoid many painful lessons. Remember how Jethro said to his son-in-law Moses, 'What you are doing is not good' (Exodus 18:17). Moses was trying to care for the people by himself and didn't realise he needed to share the responsibility, but Jethro faithfully pointed out his mistake. It was a humbling, but vital moment for Moses as he gained a new insight about his tendency to micro-manage. No wonder Proverbs says, 'Faithful are the wounds of a friend' (27:6, KJV).

I have personally been greatly helped by using *psychometric tests and other tools* that can give us insight into our personality and gifting, how we respond to conflict, what we are like under stress, and so on. None of these instruments are perfect, and none give a complete picture of who we are, but they can reveal things about us that we may not see otherwise. Often, they clarify what we already know but find hard to describe. They provide a framework for us to express ourselves and to learn about others.

I will speak later about the significant place that the Myers-Briggs Type Indicator (MBTI®) played in my life, but here it will be sufficient to say that understanding my preference for introversion (being energised mostly from within) rather than extroversion (being energised mostly from without) has been a liberating and life-giving insight. I would not have known this about myself had it not been for the

MBTI® (mistakenly thinking I had to be an extrovert) and may well have ended in burnout if I had not come to appreciate how much I need to have time and space alone to re-energise.

Finally, one practice to mention is that of *journalling*, taking the time to write down our thoughts and feelings, knowing we can be in the presence of God when doing this. This is a proven way to unpack difficult emotions and work our way through tricky situations. In a confidential notebook we can explore our most hidden thoughts and feelings, knowing that no other person will read them, and that before God they are welcomed and accepted – he knows them anyway! This kind of writing is cathartic and releases pressure, but it also helps us to clarify our thinking and take charge of any troublesome emotions. For many years I did this only occasionally, when the heat was really on, but always profitably. Re-reading my journals always helped me gain a clearer insight about myself. I can track my progress, or lack of it, and see how my thinking has changed and matured. Journalling helps me to understand and accept myself better.

Progress in the Christian life does not just happen. We apply ourselves to the call of developing our character, and part of that is to grow in self-awareness and self-understanding. Paul encourages his young protégé Timothy to 'be diligent in these matters; give yourself wholly to them, so that everyone may see your progress. Watch your life and doctrine closely' (1 Timothy 4:15–16). There are no shortcuts to maturity, and we are never too young to start paying attention to who we are, and who we are becoming.

Point of connection

This period in our discipleship journey often involves some form of training, either informally or formally, which helps to strengthen our faith and prepare us for service and potentially leadership. Learning about our faith is important, but of greater significance is what God is doing within us, especially as he begins to shape our character to carry the weight of ministry, whatever that may look like.

- How were you grounded in your understanding of the faith, and prepared to serve God at this stage in your life?

- As you read my story, what do you notice about the way God was at work in my life during this period of formal training? In what ways was this a period of preparation for me? Do you see a similar pattern in your own life?

- Why is growing in self-knowledge an essential part of spiritual formation?

- What strategies do you currently have in place to help you grow in self-awareness and self-understanding? For example, reading scripture, self-reflection, receiving feedback from trusted friends, psychometric tests, journalling, and so on. What part does Christian community play in this?

- Can you think of an example of something that was previously a 'blind-spot' for you, but now you are aware of it, and making changes?

- What part does the Holy Spirit play in your life right now? Is this sufficient?

You may wish to continue working with your timeline, now with a focus on your late teens/early 20s. Name any individuals or groups who helped you to grow in your faith.

4

PREPARING

Two are better than one, because they have a good return for their labour... A cord of three strands is not quickly broken.
ECCLESIASTES 4:9, 12

When spirituality is viewed as a journey... the way to spiritual wholeness is seen to lie in an increasingly faithful response to the one whose purpose shapes our path, whose grace redeems our detours, whose power liberates us from crippling bondages of the prior journey, and whose transforming presence meets us at each turn.
Robert Mulholland[16]

The switch in 1972 from the rarified atmosphere of Bible college to the more earthy reality of a teacher training college in Leeds was an interesting one. For example, the students smoked in lectures, drank cups of coffee, and didn't seem all that interested! No longer was I surrounded by believers, and most of my new companions had no thought of God. But it felt good to be able to live out my life in a more challenging context where there were opportunities for witness.

Preparing to teach

I was doing a one-year Postgraduate Certificate in Education (PGCE) focusing on religious and physical education. We had general lectures learning about child development and classroom management, plus specific time on our chosen subject areas. Each term involved teaching practice when we were observed by a tutor at some point. I did my first teaching at a grammar school in Otley, to the north of Leeds, and it went well, being a similar school to the one I attended. The second, in inner-city Leeds, was a much harder experience, and I was glad when it finished. I soon realised that discipline was the key issue. If you can't control the class, you can't teach much.

There was an active Christian union at the college, and I enjoyed being part of it, especially as it was the year when they held a week of mission. A well-known speaker came along and gave a series of evangelistic talks, and we created lots of opportunities to talk about faith informally in the student union. This was all very stimulating to my faith and good preparation for the future.

I spent my weekends with my parents back in Brierley. The youth group led by Dennis Bavister, and attached loosely to the chapel, had blossomed and was also experiencing the charismatic renewal. Britain had been impacted in the early 1970s by a movement of God in America, known as the Jesus People revolution, when thousands of hippies were converted to Christ.[17] There was a similar stirring in this country, especially among young people, and new ways of worship were emerging. It seemed impossible to contain this new life within the Methodist system and Dennis decided to establish a new church in the nearby village of Hemsworth where he was still a teacher, and where I had gone to school. We started meeting in a community hall and the congregation was mainly young people, with lively worship and consistent Bible teaching. I became one of the leaders and began to learn what it means to plant a church from scratch.

Confirmation of our call

Evelyn and I had become engaged the summer I finished at LBC (1972) and were planning to marry at the end of my teaching course and her time at London Bible College. We had both been involved in a young people's camp in Orkney (an island off the north coast of Scotland), and I was expecting the results of my Bachelor of Divinity exams that week. Sure enough, a message came from my mother (who had permission to open the letter with my results) to the pastor of the church where we were staying (no mobile phones then!). I had quietly said to the Lord it would be good if I could get an upper second in case I needed to do further study. The pastor came to give me the news that I had passed, and with exactly what I had hoped for, a 2:1 degree. Then, at the same moment, he handed me a magazine article he had seen about Hudson Taylor, saying, 'Here, you may like to read this, he's from your part of the world.' It seemed an amazing coincidence, a reminder from God not to forget how he was leading us. It felt like another confirmation that we were on the right track.

I enjoyed getting to know Evelyn's parents, Duncan and Mary Smith, who had a strong faith and were active members of the Baptist Church in Inverness, as well as her wider family in different parts of Scotland. Our first meeting was amusing because Evelyn's father came sporting a black eye, which he said he had received when putting out the rubbish bin on a windy day. The lid had blown back and hit him in the face. It seemed a plausible explanation, but we gave him a lot of teasing afterwards! One lovely thing was that our parents became good friends and enjoyed holidays together, despite their different backgrounds.

Life together

I completed my teacher training and Evelyn finished at college in the summer of 1973. I began looking for a job, during which time we would apply for membership of OMF. The fact that I only wanted to teach for a year was against my being given a job, but I saw an opportunity to teach R.E. and P.E. at a school in Barnsley, applied, and was given the position. They were desperate but I was delighted!

My friend Eddie (Hambleton) had bought a small, terraced house in Brierley, and was renovating it. He offered it to us at a modest rent for as long as we needed it – another provision from God. It felt like many pieces of the jigsaw were coming together and that God was in the details of our lives. We were married in early August that year in Evelyn's home church in Inverness and then went back to Yorkshire to establish our new home and prepare for the future.

I enjoyed my year of 'real' teaching, although there were some difficult classes, and I discovered that the older girls were harder to control than the boys. During R.E. lessons, I was able to introduce my pupils to the story of the local Christian hero, Hudson Taylor. I even discovered that one of the boys was a distant relative of the great man. Evelyn took a job in nursing, and we busied ourselves in the newly formed Hemsworth church, where I was now one of the elders. The first year of marriage passed quickly, then we resigned our jobs to attend the OMF candidates' course in London.

It was a daunting three-week residential event, taking in lots of information about the principles and practices of the mission, and being scrutinised in different ways to see if we were suitable for the rigours of missionary life. There was some concern about our charismatic leanings, but eventually we were accepted and told we would join the next orientation course in Singapore, starting the following January. We were excited, but the reality of what we were about to do seemed quite daunting.

The lady who ran the OMF guest house where we stayed was a formidable character, but with a heart of gold beneath her intimidating manner. She said to us one day, almost in passing, 'The missionaries who stay the longest on the field are those who have their afternoon cup of tea.' I have never forgotten those words, and although it needs some cultural adaptation, it is a piece of advice I have passed on to others many times as I have taught the principles of self-care in ministry. We should not become so busy in daily life that we cannot stop for a break.

We still had several months before our departure and needed to support ourselves. Evelyn applied for a short-term contract at a hospital specialising in mental health. I went along with her for company, but the manager who interviewed Evelyn offered me a job as well, as a ward orderly, so we both started work. He even arranged for us to have the same shift pattern, yet another example of God's extraordinary providential care. I really valued the experience and learned a lot about caring for those with mental health issues. We worked until Christmas, then had a farewell service from the Hemsworth church before saying our personal goodbyes.

Singapore

In January 1975 we left for Singapore. I was excited about the flight as I had never flown before. It was a long journey, via Bangkok. I remember stepping off the plane on arrival and feeling my face wrapped in a blanket of warm air, then smelling the tropical vegetation. I knew in that moment that I would never be the same again. This was an experience that would change my life.

We spent ten weeks in the heat of bustling Singapore, staying at the OMF headquarters, at that time a large colonial building with ceiling fans, shuttered windows, and no air conditioning. There were about 20 of us on the course, from several different nationalities and heading to various countries in Southeast Asia. We learned many things about other religions, church planting, phonetics and language learning, health in the tropics, financial matters, writing prayer letters, and so on. There were more interviews until at last we were confirmed in our appointment – Evelyn and I would go to Sarawak in east Malaysia, part of the island of Borneo, to do church planting in association with the Sidang Injil Borneo (SIB), the national evangelical church.

Prepared by God

It is so interesting looking back to see how carefully God prepared us for overseas mission, placing a strong sense of call in both our hearts that would keep us steady when our faith would be challenged through the difficulties we would inevitably face. That call was tested and confirmed by others. We had seen God provide for our needs and knew we could trust him as we joined a 'faith' mission – an organisation that did not believe in soliciting funds but in trusting God to provide. Their watchword was based on a saying of Hudson Taylor: 'God's work, done in God's way, will never lack for God's supply.' We were still young, and recently married, but had some experience in starting a church from scratch. Furthermore, we had a lot of people committed to praying for us, and we had each other.

Just before we left England, Evelyn's auntie had given me a beautiful leather Bible and inscribed in the front a verse of scripture: 'The one who calls you is faithful, and he will do it' (1 Thessalonians 5:24). This would become a constant reassurance to me over the years. Our confidence was not in ourselves, our training or giftedness, our personality or strength of character, but in the Lord. His faithfulness would carry us through on our journey of faith.

Reflection 4:

PRINCIPLES OF GUIDANCE

If we are to live a life of following God, it is obvious that we must know how to hear God's voice and receive his guidance. The Christian life is a life of being led, of following the good shepherd wherever he may lead us. That is why Jesus said, 'My sheep listen to my voice; I know them, and they follow me' (John 10:27). This implies that we can hear God's voice, but we must listen for him speaking and then be ready to respond in obedience.

This is how I have sought to live my life, and as you read my story, you will see many instances of how God has guided me, at different times and in different ways. Some aspects of this will be unique to me, but most will be held in common with anyone who desires to follow God fully. Underlying this approach is the conviction that God has a plan and purpose for each of us, and that he reveals his will to us gradually, one step at a time, over a lifetime. My assurance for this comes from Jeremiah 29:11 which says, '"For I know the plans I have for you," declares the Lord, "plans to prosper you and not to harm you, plans to give you hope and a future."' Many times this verse has spoken to me, reminding me that God has a good plan for my life, and motivating me to keep seeking his will.

The first principle of guidance is, *What does God say in his word?* The Bible reveals the will of God for us and teaches us right from wrong, so that we can choose to do what is right and avoid what is wrong. God's guidance will never contradict the clear statements about moral issues in scripture, and any guidance we receive must be in line with this. He will never, for example, ask us to steal, murder, or commit adultery.

In this way we agree with the psalmist who says, 'Your word is a lamp for my feet, a light on my path' (Psalm 119:105).

Beyond moral concerns there are also commands that give direction about how we should live our lives, which we are to apply practically through obedience and faith, submitting our own will to that of the Lord. One such general command, sometimes known as the great commission, is found in Matthew 28:19-20 where Jesus says, 'There fore go and make disciples of all nations, baptising them in the name of the Father and of the Son and of the Holy Spirit, and teaching them to obey everything I have commanded you.' This command is given to the church as a whole, but has personal application since every disciple must take this seriously and consider how it will be worked out in their own life. For me it had direct application: go to Malaysia. You will read in chapter 5 exactly how that came about, and although that specific calling turned out to be for a limited period, the sense that I am living in obedience to the great commission continued to inform everything I did and the values I have to this present moment. Not all are called to 'go' in this sense, but all are invited to play a part in fulfilling the task God has given his church – by supporting, giving, praying, and so on.

The Holy Spirit may also speak to us personally from other passages as we read, for example by applying promises to us directly, or challenging us through warnings. Again, Jesus said, 'Man shall not live on bread alone, but on every word that comes from the mouth of God' (Matthew 4:4). The word of the Lord has a way of coming to us, of finding us out and addressing us personally. At times it seems to leap off the page and speak to us directly. In my time of grief and loss (chapter 12), you will read how God brought Psalm 18:19 to my attention with the assurance that he would lead me into a spacious place. It was his reassuring word to me at a time of great need, but God will do the same thing when we are seeking guidance.

If God is to speak to us then we will need to regularly be reading and listening to scripture, with the disposition of openness shown by the boy Samuel: 'Speak, for your servant is listening' (1 Samuel 3:10).

Another principle to be aware of is, *What is God saying to you within?* The Spirit lives within us and communicates with us in our own spirit where we have the capacity to recognise his voice. This is not normally an audible voice, more usually a whisper, a sudden thought or insight, a nudge, an inner awareness, or conviction that he is speaking. Just as he testifies to our spirit that we are God's children, so he assures us of what the Father wants to say to us (Romans 8:16). For example, when Philip had been directed by an angel to follow the road down to Gaza, we read that the Spirit told him, 'Go to that chariot and stay near it' (Acts 8:29). By obeying the inner voice he met an Ethiopian official, led him to Christ, and then baptised him. Every disciple has the same ability to hear God speak to them. We have been given 'ears to hear' (Mark 4:9) and must pay close attention to the voice of God, becoming familiar with his quiet whispers. This is a life-long discipline and essential if we are to follow God's leading.

Then we can consider the question, *What is on your heart to do?* God has designed us to do his will, and we carry within us a sense of destiny, of God-given purpose, which when we are surrendered to God comes to the fore in our thinking. It is good to give attention to the desires in our hearts, godly ambitions that he has planted there to bring glory to God. Psalm 37:4 says, 'Take delight in the Lord, and he will give you the desires of your heart.' The desire that Evelyn and I had to serve in Malaysia was a God-given desire, a calling confirmed by the leadership of the mission and affirmed by our church. We should not be afraid of such godly ambitions, but take note of them and share our thinking with wise friends and leaders to help us discern the way ahead.

Then we can consider, *Is the way opening up?* This is the principle of the open or closed door. If God is leading us in a particular direction, then we can expect the way to open ahead of us. Circumstances will come together to make it possible. It is said of Jesus, 'What he opens no one can shut, and what he shuts no one can open' (Revelation 3:7). The apostle Paul wrote that in Ephesus 'a great door for effective work has opened to me' (1 Corinthians 16:9); Paul saw a God-given opportunity and took hold of it.

At the same time, we may experience a door closing, as when much later we were unable to return to Malaysia (see chapter 6). Paul also knew this disappointment when, thinking it was right to go into Bithynia he was restrained by the Spirit from going there. Then, through a dream, he received clear confirmation to enter Macedonia (Acts 16:6–10). Often, when one door closes, another unexpectedly opens. Without God's intervention we may have followed our own plans and missed what he had in mind for us. So, we can ask, 'Is the door open or closed?'

A final question is, *Can I see the hand of God in this?* In my experience, much of my guidance has been providential, by which I mean that God has guided me almost without my awareness, arranging the circumstances of my life to bring me to the right place at the right time. He has caused me to meet significant people who were like gatekeepers, leading me into new ministry opportunities. We should always be alert to unusual coincidences, things that just seem to happen as if by chance but in reality occur in the planning of God. In the story of Ruth, I love how when she went out to glean, she just happened to find herself working in the field belonging to Boaz, a distant relative and the one who would redeem them and be the man she would marry. A God-incidence not a coincidence (Ruth 2:3)!

Discerning God's will can sometimes be confusing, and often we are called to wait for the way to become clear. Yet, if our sincere intention is to do his will, he will eventually make the way plain. Often, bringing our will into alignment with his will is the crucial first step in guidance. We must surrender what we want, to do what he wants. Then, if we cry out to him, he will surely lead us: 'Show me your ways, Lord, teach me your paths' (Psalm 25:4). Guidance need not be a baffling puzzle.

God wants to reveal his will to us and will speak if we are humbly listening: 'Good and upright is the Lord; therefore he instructs sinners in his ways. He guides the humble in what is right and teaches them his way' (Psalm 25:8–9).

Point of connection

When we are starting out in adult life, we have many crucial decisions to make, such as what career we should follow, whether we should marry or not, and where we might be located. We could decide these things according to our own wisdom or, more wisely, ask God to guide us in our decision-making. If we have surrendered ourselves to the love of God, then we can be open to whatever he has in mind for us without fear. We know that we were made to do his will and, in discovering that, we find the purpose for which we were made. In that place lies our true happiness.

- How do you best hear the voice of God? In what ways does God normally speak to you?

- As you read my story, how did God confirm our call to mission? Why is it important to have assurance about such a calling?

- Not all are called to Christian ministry, and not all are called to cross-cultural mission, but we each have a part to play in the great commission. How is that expressed in your life?

- One of the names for God is Jehovah-Jireh, which means 'the Lord will provide' (Genesis 22:14). When God calls us to a task, he provides all we need, when we need it. This is a lesson we often learn in the early days of following Jesus, but one which we continue to learn throughout our journey. Reflect on the times you have experienced this. How does this strengthen your faith?

- In what ways have you been guided by God in your decision-making? Consider the principles of guidance given here – how do they compare with your own experience? What advice would you give to a young person seeking God's will in a major decision?

You may like to add to your timeline any major movements in your life made in response to God's guidance.

5
SERVING

You did not choose me, but I chose you and appointed you so that you might go and bear fruit – fruit that will last.

JOHN 15:16

Jesus said his disciples are to be servants. Being a servant is part of what it means to be a Christian leader. Our leader came not to be served, but to serve. We are to do the same.

Bill Hull[18]

Before we could start our ministry, there was still more training and preparation. We went from Singapore to Miri, a small coastal town in east Malaysia, bordering the South China Sea, and well known for its oil industry. OMF had recently merged with the Borneo Evangelical Mission (BEM) and had established their headquarters in Miri, a largely Chinese town with good transport and communication links.

Settling in

We were seven new recruits and spent three months there doing Malay language study but also being introduced to the local customs and cultures, as well as the history of the Sidang Injil Borneo (SIB) church with whom we would be working. We were fortunate that Hudson Southwell, one of the original pioneer missionaries, was still living in Miri and we could hear stirring first-hand accounts of how God had worked in the early days in what was a significant movement amongst the Lun Bawang and Kelabit peoples.[19]

Evelyn and I had two trips into the interior to familiarise ourselves with life in the jungle. The first was to Long Atip, a Kayan village at the head of the mighty River Baram. It was our first experience of life in a longhouse, a sort of village on stilts measured by the number of 'doors' or families. In Long Atip there were about 90 such doors, families living in close community, each with a separate living space but sharing a common veranda where people gathered to work or socialise. Decisions were made communally under the leadership of a headman, and a unique feature of the conversion of many villages in the interior of Borneo was that they decided to follow Christ as a whole group. Beneath the longhouse, a wooden structure built off the ground on stilts, was space for chickens and pigs. Cooking was by kerosene stove, and lighting by tilly lamp. The only access was by river, where people went to bathe, do their washing, and catch fish. Life was simple, and since the whole village had turned to Christ, there were regular church services on the veranda.

We were escorted by Sylvia Webb, a senior missionary fluent in the Kayan language, and we stayed with Anyi, a teacher in the village school. I remember going down to the river to cool off one hot afternoon, and sitting there in the water, surrounded by tall jungle trees, feeling, 'This is what I was made for.' Very few of the children had seen white people and whenever we approached, they ran away to hide, but the adults made a fuss of us. It was a great experience.

We also spent a couple of weeks at the SIB headquarters in a rural town called Lawas. This was the base for the mission plane, radio studio, and a Bible school. Again, we were learning to live in simple conditions, develop our Malay language skills, and get to know the leaders of the SIB. It was still strange and unfamiliar to us, and we were happy when we got back to 'civilisation' in Miri with electricity and familiar foods.

Moving to Kuching

Our three months of language and orientation eventually passed, and it was agreed that we would move down to Kuching, the capital of the state of Sarawak. There a fledgling church was developing with young people who had moved from the interior villages into the city to be trained as teachers, nurses, and agriculturalists. Our job would be to disciple the new believers and develop leaders. Although I would be their pastor, the aim was to work myself out of a job, in line with Paul's advice to Timothy: 'The things you have heard me say in the presence of many witnesses entrust to reliable people who will also be qualified to teach others' (2 Timothy 2:2). This was a principle of ministry with which I heartily agreed, and one which has shaped my approach to ministry ever since. As leaders we are called to help God's people discover their gifts and to provide opportunities for them to use them. We are to release others into leadership positions and delight in seeing them flourish. In other words, we are to multiply ourselves, and in mission terms, work ourselves out of a job.

Kuching in the 1970s was a beautiful town, just north of the equator, built alongside the slow-moving, coffee-coloured River Sarawak, as it winds its way lazily to the sea. Lush tropical vegetation abounded, with shady trees and brightly coloured flowers. Malay, Chinese, and colonial buildings gave it a sense of history and architectural variety. There was always something interesting (and unusual) to see in the vibrant market or when browsing the shops. Mountains in the distance provided a beautiful panorama and the pace of life was slow and gentle, like the river and the people. We fell in love with it at once.

It was the people who grabbed my heart the most. We had a young congregation, mostly students and not-yet-married couples, but they were keen to learn and eager to grow in their faith. They welcomed us warmly. I couldn't wait to get started, but I made an early mistake that could have jeopardised the whole thing. I had not yet grasped the subtle difference between western and Asian cultures, especially when it comes to 'losing face' (being shamed publicly), so when I corrected a couple of the young men over a small matter, they were highly offended. According to one of them, it took them two years before they forgave me.

Learning to lead

I came in for some criticism too in the early days, for which I was unprepared. I wrote in my despair for some advice from a friend back home who had a lot of ministry experience. He replied tersely, 'Criticism is God's sandpaper to smooth our rough edges. The man who never made a mistake never made anything.' I simply had to learn from my mistakes and get on with it. In the end we won through, because people were very gracious, saw that we really loved them, and took us to their hearts.

Relational learning (how to lead people) is a key aspect in the early days of what Dr J. Robert Clinton calls the 'ministry maturing' phase. He says, 'Conflict is a powerful tool in the hand of God and can be used to teach a leader lessons that he would not learn any other way… Ministry conflict, like general conflict, tests a leader's personal maturity. What we truly are is revealed in a crisis.'[20] Conflict is inevitable throughout life, but perhaps even more likely when we are working cross-culturally. This was my first experience of it, but it would not be the last.

My gift of teaching seemed to be appreciated, and I loved every opportunity to explain the gospel, teach the Bible story, and show people how to grow as a Christian. I feel my real ability as a teacher is to make complicated things simple and easy to understand, and this was important in a context where we used English, but where it was not the first language of most of the congregation. I learnt to speak slowly, clearly, and to avoid idioms or unfamiliar words. I used illustrations from the local context and began to understand the Malaysian sense of humour which was important in connecting with my listeners.

Growth

The church met in the large open space beneath the house where we lived, which was fine in good weather, but in the wet season it would often be a case of 'rain stopped play' – the service, anyway. I loved the worship as people sang joyfully and with such natural harmonies, even when accompanied by nothing more than a guitar. They responded eagerly to the gospel as well, and a steady stream of young people were converted. We started a class for new believers, and a Bible study for more established believers on Saturday afternoons, which was followed by a prayer meeting.

A distinctive feature of the Kuching church was the desire to reach out with the gospel, especially to the Iban and Bedayuh groups in the surrounding countryside. Regular teams went out at weekends to stay in the villages and teach people, who had animastic beliefs, about Jesus. Gradually new churches came into being and people were set free from demonic bondages and witchcraft. It was exciting stuff, and we had to be on our toes. We discovered the reality of spiritual warfare, and the need to wear the full armour of God, as described by Paul in Ephesians 6:10–20.

Family life

It was during this period that our two children were born. Alistair was the first to arrive in 1976, and then Debbie in 1978, which meant we had two small children to care for with no family support, except that we had a house helper and lots of young people willing to babysit and give us a break from time to time. Living and working in the tropics was very tiring, but we were careful to take Mondays as a day of rest and the mission made sure we took annual leave in the cool of the Cameron Highlands over in west Malaysia.

Inevitably, in a church of young people, there were weddings and soon followed babies. We started a kindergarten for these young ones and as an outreach to other young families. We opened a bookshop and sold Christian literature. Gradually older people joined us, and we welcomed back several who had been overseas to study, been converted, and now wanted to be involved in church life in their home country. Several of these developed into our emerging leadership team and were a great asset. Those who had been students graduated and took on important jobs in government departments, the hospitals, and local schools. Their first posting was often 'outstation', to the remoter jungle areas, and they infectiously took the gospel with them. It was all so exciting.

Home assignment

In April 1978 we returned to England for our first furlough. After four years away, and now with two children, we couldn't wait to see our families. When they met us at the airport there was much excitement, but when I turned to look at Alistair, now two years old, he looked lost. I am ashamed to say this now, but we hadn't realised for him this was not coming home but rather arriving in a strange country; and these people who wanted to make a fuss of him were strangers. We knew nothing about transition and change, nor about the challenges of being a child brought up in another culture (often called Third Culture Kids or TCKs). Nowadays people are much better prepared for coping with change and there is a lot of support for families in transition (see the reflection in chapter 11).

We had a full year on furlough, reconnecting with our home churches in Yorkshire and Scotland, doing deputation meetings to share about the church in Sarawak in various places, and taking part in some missionary conferences. We lived with my parents in Brierley mostly, but also at times with Evelyn's parents in Inverness. It was a good time, but we were ready to return to our 'other' home in Kuching.

Second term

The Kuching church had done well in our absence and had continued to grow. The leaders had matured and were working well together, leading services, and preaching regularly. A really valuable addition to the church was the arrival of Balan Seling, a widely respected Christian leader who was also a member of Parliament. When revival broke out in the Kelabit Highlands in 1975 it was Balan who gave wise counsel that allowed for the work of the Spirit without excesses. His presence in the Kuching church was a stabilising influence.

We had expected to continue our ministry in Kuching, but in 1980 were asked to move back to Miri to deputise for the field leader, Brian Michell, who was due to return to New Zealand for leave. I did not want to do this as I was very happy in my role in Kuching, but OMF described itself then as 'a benign dictatorship' (a term coined by Oswald Sanders when he was general director), and it was expected that the needs of the work as a whole came before individual preferences. We acquiesced, but somewhat reluctantly, as I didn't feel this new role played to my strengths.

There was a lot to learn, and it was a big step up from being one of the missionary team to being responsible for the well-being and direction of much older colleagues. A lot of the job was basic administration, which I managed adequately, and there were regular meetings to attend with the leaders of the SIB (which tested my language ability since they were held in Malay), but again I coped reasonably well.

One big task on my to-do list was the sale of the mission aircraft which was now underused and sitting idle in the hanger in Lawas. I had no idea how to do this and asked for much prayer. Miraculously, another mission in the Philippines said they wanted to buy it and would fly it out, if the engine would start, and if they deemed it safe. Otherwise, we would have to arrange for it to be taken by boat. Again, much prayer. Their staff came over, got it going, and off it went. I was so relieved and consider it one of my best answers to prayer!

There is no doubt that my leadership gift was sharpened during this year in Miri when I was forced to broaden my horizons and learn new skills. I was given opportunity for leadership training over in Singapore which made me feel valued within the mission. There were also opportunities to preach at various conferences in both English and Malay, and to teach at the local Bible college in Miri, so I was growing in that area as well. It is always good to submit ourselves to the direction of colleagues, and to learn submission, even if it doesn't sit easily with our own preferences. As my time there came to an end, I received a beautiful handwritten note from Jim Taylor, then OMF's international director, saying how well I had done, and thanking me for being willing to move.

The move to Sibu

From Miri, we were asked to relocate to Sibu, an inland town where our friends Brian and Esther Newton had done a great job in leading a similar congregation to the one in Kuching. They were also going back on home assignment for a year, and we were asked to fill in for them, which we did willingly.

Sibu felt like a very different place to Kuching, however, being predominantly Foochow Chinese, and with a strong Methodist history. Built alongside the mighty River Rejang, it was the hub for river traffic going far into the interior as well as to the coast and the South China Sea. The church reflected this cultural background, being mostly English-speaking Chinese rather than indigenous people. We were made to feel welcome though and, as we settled in, began to get to know the new congregation and to assess their needs.

One personal issue loomed large in our minds, however – schooling for Alistair, who had now turned five. The mission policy was for children to attend Chefoo School over in the Cameron Highlands in Peninsular Malaysia, and the plan was for him to go too. We knew the school very well, and it offered an excellent education and a loving, caring environment. The staff were experienced in helping children through the separation, and they would come home at the end of each term. Still, it was a big ask for him, and for us. With no viable alternative, we agreed that he should go and began to prepare him for this major transition in his young life.

Alistair did well at the school. We wrote to him every week, and sent photos, and his Dorm Auntie helped him write to us, sent photos, and kept us up to date on his progress. He settled easily, did well academically, and enjoyed all the out-of-class activities. As far as we could tell he did not suffer too much from homesickness. But we missed him, and so did his sister, Debbie. Nowadays people would be reluctant to allow their children to leave home at such a young age, and rightly so. Knowing what we know now about child development, we would not do that again, but it is the way things were then, and what was expected of us. One lovely memory – my father, who hardly wrote a letter in his life, wrote faithfully almost weekly to this special grandson all the time he was at Chefoo.

The Sibu congregation had always been more open to the work of the Spirit than the Kuching one, and we found them hungry to grow in God. We worked alongside Betty Lau, a young Chinese girl gifted in evangelism and with a great sense of humour. She had a real burden for her Chinese-speaking relatives and eventually started a service for them. The church had recently purchased a building of its own, which was used as an outreach centre and the location for a Christian bookshop. We started a class for new believers which quickly gained momentum, and the church was healthy and buoyant.

The year in Sibu passed quickly and we were sad to leave, but in April 1983 it was time for our second home assignment. Alistair came back from Chefoo, and as a family we left for England. This time we had our own house, a rented property quite near to my parents in Yorkshire. Both Alistair and Debbie started at the local primary school, and after a period of adjustment, felt at home in their new surroundings.

We had a feeling of satisfaction as we looked back on our second term, with its many adjustments and challenges, but had no idea that a major blow was soon to come our way that would turn our world upside down.

Reflection 5:

SERVANT MINISTRY

Our time in Malaysia provided me with my first experience of real leadership. Yes, I had been an elder in the fledgling Hemsworth church, but in Sarawak I had responsibility for a whole congregation for the first time. I was young and green (only 26 when we moved to Kuching) with a lot to learn, and of course I made mistakes.

OMF had entered into a partnership with the Borneo Evangelical Mission (BEM) and we worked under their umbrella. The BEM's philosophy was that the mission was like the scaffolding surrounding a new building. Once the building was complete, the scaffolding should be removed – in other words, when the national church was ready, leadership and resources should be handed over to them, and any missionaries would work under national leadership. We were to work ourselves out of a job. Those of us in local church ministry were tasked to develop younger leaders who would be able to lead the town congregations. This meant that training others was a top priority. It also meant that we were called to serve, to use our gifts to build the national church, not to create a position or platform for ourselves. Ever since then my philosophy of ministry has been one which can best be described as servant ministry.

Christian leadership, based as it is upon the example of Jesus, is about serving others and not lording it over them. Jesus said simply and clearly, 'I am among you as one who serves' (Luke 22:27). He made it clear to his disciples that in his kingdom the one who rules is the one who serves, and that there should be no jockeying for position or dominating of others. The apostle Paul followed a similar approach:

'For what we preach is not ourselves, but Jesus Christ as Lord, and ourselves as your servants for Jesus' sake' (2 Corinthians 4:5). Sadly, this has not always been the style of leadership found in churches and Christian organisations.

Servant leadership is to lead in God's way with humility and gentleness, recognising that any leadership ability we have is a gift from him which we gladly exercise on behalf of others as our way of serving the body of Christ. This may well run contrary to the cultural norms of leadership that we are used to, and our own assumptions that servants do not normally lead; but it is the way of Jesus.

All leadership rightly involves the exercise of authority and power, and if this is done wisely and with a servant heart, there is no problem. However, it is always open to abuse and misuse by insecure and ambitious leaders. In response to a spate of leadership scandals in Britain, where abuses of power and position have occurred, Marcus Honeysett has written about what he terms the slippery slope of power: 'the path that runs from good intentions, via lack of accountability and transparency, down into manipulation and self-serving, all the way to the most serious abuses'.[21] The examples he gives range from hurtful behaviour to harassment, coercive and dominating leadership, and even criminal physical and/or sexual abuse.

How then can we encourage and develop a more Christ-centred approach to leadership and guard against the abuse of authority?

Firstly, by emphasising in all leadership training that character takes precedence over giftedness. Spiritual formation should therefore be a priority and the development of the inner life given a special place in leadership training. The characteristics of good leadership we seek to emulate are those seen clearly in Jesus, who described himself as 'gentle and humble in heart' (Matthew 11:29).

Gentleness refers to the way we treat other people, showing them dignity and respect and recognising their intrinsic worth and value. How we deal with the weak and vulnerable, the wayward and the slow to respond, the bruised and the hurting will be vital. Servant leaders are motivated by love and compassion, and their care and concern shines through and is expressed in patience and forbearance.

Humility is the opposite of pride and self-ambition, of boasting and self-promotion. Humble leaders do not set themselves above others but treat others with equality. In particular, humility is expressed as dependency on God and the willingness to receive help from others. Humble leaders give glory to God and claim nothing for themselves. They are willing to listen to the views of others, receive constructive feedback, and recognise they may not have all the answers. They realise they have limitations and are only human.

Secondly, we can encouarge and develop a more Christ-centred approach to leadership by helping potential leaders to grow in self-awareness (see chapter 3) and to be willing to seek healing for any woundedness they may bring with them from their past. Poor leadership is often fuelled by insecurity and the need to achieve as proof of one's worth and value. Wounded leaders are often driven, overly ambitious, and cannot take criticism or receive even helpful feedback without a strong negative reaction. They may be high achievers but show a tendency to steam-roller other people to achieve their goals. Those leaders who have experienced trauma in the past may find themselves triggered by present stressful circumstances and respond in unhelpful and unhealthy ways, re-enacting their past and damaging the present.

Leadership formation must therefore provide potential leaders with the opportunity to talk through painful issues from the past and receive professional counselling if necessary. As we receive the love of God through times of prayer and ministry, and as we increasingly find our identity as God's deeply loved children, we can find freedom and release from destructive patterns that impact our relationships and ability to lead well.

Thirdly, we should place an emphasis on genuine ongoing account-ability with a mentor, leadership coach, spiritual director, or such like. This only works if there is the willingness to be open and transparent on the part of the leader, and if a high degree of trust is present. Increasingly, whole denominations (like the Methodist Church in Britain) are introducing compulsory supervision for ministers, which can only be helpful. Of course, this must be offered in a safe and grace-filled context, not one filled with judgement and condemnation. People can only be authentic if they are sure they are safe and will not be penalised for their vulnerability.

It must be recognised that leaders themselves can be abused by church members or people in the organisations that they serve and there is still much work to be done in helping congregations to care well for the leaders who serve them.[22] We are all called to be servants and to develop environments where people are loved, honoured, and treated with respect.

One resistance to the idea of servant leadership that is often expressed is that it is weak leadership. If leaders are servants, will they be treated like a dogsbody, generally taken advantage of and loaded with all the menial tasks that no one else wants to do? Certainly, leaders need to be assertive and have clear boundaries, remembering that they are first serving God and are answerable to him. They need to have a clear sense of what they are called to do, and what they are not called to do. They need to be able to say 'No' as well as 'Yes' to requests for their time. The servant style of leadership is no excuse for passivity or cowardly behaviour.

Another concern is whether servant leaders will be able to lead with authority and conviction, providing clear vision and direction, if they are too kind and gentle. For sure, they must not shy away from exercising visionary leadership, but they can provide this in a collaborative, consensus-based, and inclusive way that makes it *our* vision (shared by the group) not simply *my* vision (imposed by the leader). This may involve a slower process but will create a greater ownership which will ultimately lead to a more lasting accomplishment.

One of the greatest leaders of recent times was the Anglican vicar and author John Stott. Internationally revered as a speaker and writer, Stott gave himself to developing other leaders and was known by countless people whom he had mentored simply as 'Uncle John'. The vicar of a large and influential church in central London, he epitomised the characteristics of a true servant in his humility and graciousness and wrote this: 'At every stage of our Christian development and in every sphere of our Christian discipleship, pride is the great enemy and humility our greatest friend.'[23]

This is a vital truth to remember as we seek to grow in our own servanthood.[24]

Point of connection

Training and preparation for ministry can take a long time, and requires patience and an understanding of the process. There is always a danger that we rush into things before we are ready. Even then we will make mistakes and will still be wearing our 'L' plates. Great humility is needed.

- Think back over your own entrance into ministry or service. Were you impatient to get started? What learning process did you go through to equip you for your calling?

- I speak here about 'relational learning' as being a key development point during this phase. What do you understand by the term? What have you learned about relating to other people in the context of ministry?

- Another key learning point at this stage is that of submission to authority. This can be a hard lesson to learn but is an indicator of how well we will exercise authority ourselves. How did that work out in my case? How has it been worked out in your own life?

- Hudson Taylor, the founder of OMF, established a principle of 'moving men for God through prayer alone'. Did you notice a significant answer to prayer in my narrative? How has your own confidence in prayer been formed? Why is it important for us to be people of prayer?

- What is your response to the reflection on servant ministry? Is this something you aspire to in your own leadership? What abuses of leadership authority have you come across, and what can you learn from such sad episodes? How might you protect yourself from the slippery slope of power abuse?

On your timeline you may like to consider and mark key moments and events during your 30s (if you've reached your 30s).

6

TESTING

Consider it pure joy, my brothers and sisters, whenever you face trials of many kinds, because you know that the testing of your faith produces perseverance. Let perseverance finish its work so that you may be mature and complete, not lacking in anything.

JAMES 1:2–4

For maturity purposes the most important thing learned is the awareness of one's own character.

DR J. ROBERT CLINTON[25]

Trials come in many forms. Some test our integrity, asking if we will be faithful, honest, and true. Others test our mettle, asking if we have the depth of character to endure hardship and to keep going despite disappointments and setbacks. God allows such trials to come because they wean us away from self-dependency and pride, and, if we respond well, they can help us to depend more fully on God.

Those trials which test our character are used by God to develop in us perseverance, a quality which we might now call resilience. Difficulties shape who we are, bringing us to maturity and a more grown-up faith that is not dependent on everything going well but one which can endure and trust God even in the darkness. This is what James is teaching us in the verses quoted above. The next few years in my journey proved to be a season of testing, greater than anything I had experienced before.

A door closes

As far as we knew, after our home assignment, we would continue to work with OMF in Sarawak. We felt we were in the mission for life, so were surprised when, in early 1984, we heard that we would not be welcomed back. It was a total shock, and we were never quite sure what the reasoning was behind the decision. Perhaps someone had taken exception to the association of our home church with the house church movement that was impacting the UK in the 1980s, fearing we would be a conduit for such radical teachings into the SIB. There was a suggestion also that my gathering together of younger leaders for a conference in Sibu during our time there was an attempt on my part to gain a following for myself. Neither allegation was correct.

We tried to reason with the mission, but they stuck to their decision, leaving us without a job and with a young family to care for, and at very short notice. When it was announced in our home church that we would not be returning to Malaysia, the whole congregation burst into applause – they were glad we would be staying – whereas I burst into tears. I felt that I had been robbed of one of the most precious things in my life, and I was devastated. I felt like a failure, and deeply ashamed, as if I had done something wrong. It seemed unjust and unfair, and I wondered what people would think of me.

A door opens

Our home church was very supportive of us. The congregation had grown considerably during our absence and was now meeting in two venues – Hemsworth and Barnsley. It was suggested that I become leader of the Hemsworth church (the original congregation) and that

Dennis Bavister, while in overall leadership, would focus on the newer work in Barnsley. In retrospect, I should have taken more time to think through my options, but I was at such a low point I thought no one would want me as their pastor, and it seemed the safest option, so we agreed.

Our churches were linked into a growing network of churches in the north of England under the name 'Harvestime', which was led by brothers Bryn and Keri Jones. They were designated as apostles and worked in partnership with a team of other men identified as prophets, evangelists, pastors, and teachers (Ephesians 4:11) overseeing the churches in their care. This recognition of the present-day validity of all the ministry gifts mentioned by Paul was what gave them the name 'Restoration movement'. They believed in a recovery of all the gifts of the Spirit and a return to the New Testament pattern for church life. The platform for their teaching was the Dales Bible Week, held annually in Harrogate, a time of rich worship, celebration, and powerful Bible teaching. I have to say that I had never experienced such a combination of word and Spirit before, and I was carried along in the fervour associated with a new move of God.

Hemsworth was a mining village, and in a depressed state during the Miners' Strike in 1984. As a church we did our best to help some of our members who were out on strike, supporting them financially and pastorally. I met weekly with a small group of men who were in this position for Bible study and fellowship, and not only did we see their needs being met, but they grew rapidly in God. One of that group eventually went into full-time ministry, and his spiritual journey eventually led him to the Anglican Church.

Although the church grew, and we had many happy times, I did not find it an easy church to lead. This was the church that had been formed out of a group of young people, and was mainly youngish families, but there seemed to be a lot of rivalry and jockeying for position. We had a very modern church building, and they had sacrificed a great deal of their time and money in building the church (literally), mostly by themselves. However, the pressure had left its mark on them. While they knew freedom in the Spirit, there was also a strong legalistic strand in their discipleship from the involvement with Harvestime, expressed in the necessity for women to wear head coverings and in an unhealthy submission to authority.

The links between the two churches remained strong and together we opened a Christian school, based in the Barnsley building. There was a strong feeling at the time that state education was becoming more anti-Christian, and that to protect our children we should teach them ourselves in an environment where they could also be taught Christian values. The members of both congregations were encouraged to send their children to the new school, and almost all did, withdrawing their children from the state system.

A time to stand

Eventually cracks began to appear in the relationship between our two churches and the Harvestime leaders, and Dennis decided to pull out of Harvestime, which meant we at the Hemsworth church had to follow as well. I was more concerned by what I saw within our own two churches. By this time, I was becoming increasingly troubled by what felt to me like a heavy-handed approach to discipline and a rigid pattern of discipleship which caused many people to suffer because they did not toe the party line. Many people in both congregations seemed to live in fear, a fear of man rather than of God. Our involvement in the school made matters worse because there was no boundary between church and school. If someone was not doing well in church, it could affect their children in school; if children were not doing well in school, it would become a church matter. Without the covering provided by the Harvestime leaders, we felt vulnerable.

In the end it became a matter of conscience for me. I could no longer go along with what I saw happening around me, and realised I had to make a stand. My first thought was simply to leave, although I knew no one left easily and without pain. But my thoughts were for the congregation in Hemsworth, who would be left without a pastor. Was I a hireling or a true shepherd? When one of the elders from the Barnsley church shared his own concerns with me, we recognised the time had come to take a stand and confront the issue.

As we anticipated, our attempt to deal with the problem did not go well, and the whole thing blew up in our faces. In the end we decided as a church to go our own way, which was a relief to many. It was not an easy parting of the ways, and for sure I did not handle things well, because the fear factor was massive and made it hard to respond to the situation calmly. It was not the outcome I had hoped for, but as I have thought about it since, I realise that it was probably inevitable, and maybe needed to happen.

It took me a long time to recover from this. Who wants to cause division in the church, even if it is for a just cause? I felt guilty and deeply bruised. I should have sought counselling, because it was a traumatic experience, but that didn't occur to me, so I battled on with little opportunity to talk about my experience. There were occasional attempts to reconcile with Dennis, but it was clear that any reconciliation would only happen if I repented and acknowledged I was wrong. That I could not do. Although I deeply regretted the loss of the relationship, I sincerely believed (and still do) that I had no other option. I remain truly grateful for all that Dennis contributed to my early discipleship, but this was a moment when I had to stand firm in what I believed.

Rebuilding

Rebuilding the Hemsworth congregation took time, and with the shackles of legalism now off there were some who went too far in their freedom, but gradually we developed a new equilibrium and found a new identity. In particular – and this is perhaps the upside of what happened – I would say that I 'fell into grace'. All the time I had been at Hemsworth, I kept feeling that we lacked a true understanding of grace and of Christian liberty; although charismatic, we were still under the law. With help from different quarters, I began to explore the true meaning of grace as God's unconditional love, and how that awareness impacted on Christian behaviour and discipleship. I knew I needed that discovery for myself before I could lead others into it. One person who helped me immensely was the singer, Dave Bilbrough.

I had always enjoyed Dave's music, with its emphasis on grace. We invited him to come to Hemsworth and teach on worship as well as share in the church. I took to him immediately, finding him authentic and living out what he sang. A friendship developed and I invited him to join me on a trip to Malaysia where he would lead worship and I would preach.

On the long plane journey out to Kuching I shared my story with him and plied him with questions. Dave was from the charismatic stream too, but his style of church was less authoritarian and not at all legalistic. Our conversations were so healing to me, and I realised I was not alone in my growing understanding of grace. The whole purpose of Paul's letter to the Galatians is to counteract the tendency of the church to fall back under the law, a tendency that must be resisted. Paul is unequivocal: 'It is for freedom that Christ has set us free. Stand firm, then, and do not let yourselves be burdened again by a yoke of slavery' (Galatians 5:1).

We are not to use our freedom, though, as an excuse for sinful or fleshly behaviour. Just as we are to shun legalism, we must not exchange liberty for licence. Rather, we are to live by the Spirit, putting to death those sinful tendencies within us, and then allowing ourselves to be led by the Spirit so that we produce the lovely fruit of the Spirit in our lives. Each day we are to walk in step with the Spirit, responding to his promptings and keeping a clear conscience. That is the way we fulfil the law, at least as I understand Galatians 5:13–26. The message of grace revolutionised my own life and has been the inspiration for my teaching ever since.

How extraordinary that I should make such a discovery when it felt like the bottom had fallen out of my world. Yet isn't that how God often works to prepare us for something new? It is when we have come to an end of ourselves that we are most receptive to God's ability to work within us and use us in our weakness. Perhaps we should not be surprised by this, but who would choose such painful learning?

Reflection 6:

DISAPPOINTED WITH GOD?

We all know what it feels like when things don't go according to plan. Life seldom works out exactly as we expect, and even when we think we are doing God's will, and have prayerfully committed our way to him, we may still experience setbacks, reversals, and undesirable outcomes that leave us frustrated and disappointed – often with God. Why, when we are seeking to please him, does he allow such things to happen?

You will easily identify in my own story moments when I have been disappointed with God and left feeling confused and bewildered when things didn't work out as I expected. It is not wrong to feel such emotions. Mary and Martha, the sisters from Bethany who enjoyed such a close relationship with Jesus, were left baffled and upset when Jesus delayed coming to them when Lazarus was ill. After his death, they both said the same thing directly to Jesus: 'Lord, if you had been here, my brother would not have died' (John 11:21, 32). Think, too, of the dejection felt by the two friends on the Emmaus road after the crucifixion of Jesus: 'We had hoped that he was the one who was going to redeem Israel' (Luke 24:21).

You will no doubt be able to add your own experience of disappointment – a job offer that didn't materialise, a child who has gone astray, the expectation of being married that remains unfulfilled, the sudden and tragic loss of a loved one, a friendship terminated, a church that has torn itself apart through infighting, and so on.

How can we come to terms with such disappointment in our walk with God? I have no definitive answer to give, only some glimpses of what may be happening and some simple responses we can make.

We can *talk openly with God* about our pain and our frustrations. We need not blame God, but we are certainly encouraged in the scriptures to express our emotions before him. Many of the Psalms are songs of lament, sad songs where the singer sings the blues following disappointment and confusion. And remember the cry of Jesus on the cross, echoing the experience of the psalmist: 'My God, my God, why have you forsaken me' (Psalm 22:1, Matthew 27:46)?

We may need to *adjust our expectations of God*. Faith is not an insurance policy against misfortune, nor a guarantee of a trouble-free life. God is more concerned about our holiness than our happiness, and this life was never meant to satisfy us. Indeed, our sufferings make us yearn for something better, the life which is still to come. Jesus was clear that a life of discipleship will not be easy: 'In this world you will have trouble. But take heart! I have overcome the world' (John 16:33).

Perhaps *it is life that is unfair, not God*. We live in a world that has been marred by the entrance of sin and is not as God intended it to be. Bad things happen to good people. Believers are caught up in natural disasters, experience the evil of human nature, get sick, and die like anyone else. It is natural to want to blame somebody for our misfortunes, but sometimes blaming is not the answer. Life happens and it can be unkind, but God is always there to comfort us in our distress.

A surprising truth is that disappointment, and suffering in general, can be *a key part of our spiritual formation*. God may use our pain to shape us, creating in us a deeper dependency on him, and allowing our pain to make us humbler and more compassionate. Suffering is necessary for the growth of the soul. This is what Paul is teaching us in Romans 5:3–4 when he writes, 'We also glory in our sufferings, because we know that suffering produces perseverance; perseverance, character;

and character, hope.' In other words, we become more resilient in life simply because we have faced hardship and misfortune.

The difficulties of life provide us with the opportunity to *develop a deeper trust in God* and to learn how to live by faith, not by sight (2 Corinthians 5:7). When our self-sufficiency is exposed as inadequate and we are brought to the end of our own resources, we have no alternative but to turn to God for help. At such moments he does not fail us but meets us in our place of brokenness. If we could always understand what is happening to us, we would have no need to trust in God. Faith comes to the fore when we can't see ahead of us, when darkness surrounds us. We can choose to trust in God's word, his promises to us, and the goodness of his character even when circumstances and feelings seem to contradict what we know to be true. This kind of naked faith glorifies God and delights his heart.

Finally, disappointment and confusion introduce us to *the mystery of God*, reminding us that as finite human beings we can never fathom the purpose of God (Proverbs 3:5-6, Romans 11:33-66, 1 Corinthians 13:11-12). If our minds could comprehend all the ways of God we would be as wise as he is, but we are not. By recognising our lack of understanding we are acknowledging that God is greater than we are and his ways are beyond our understanding. We end up eventually with a bigger view of God.

There are some things we can do during a time of disappointment that may help us weather the storm. It may be helpful to talk with a counsellor or spiritual director, and in a safe space to talk honestly about our pain, confusion, and doubt. Sometimes giving voice to our concerns is a way of taking hold of troublesome emotions and regaining a sense of proportion. Processing what has happened with the help of a skilled listener can play a significant part on the path to recovery.

We can also receive prayer ministry for any hurt we may carry. The Holy Spirit has a gentle way of bringing healing and peace to us, even during difficult circumstances.

Some may be helped by reading. Pete Greig's *God on Mute* (Gospel Light Publications, 2012) is a wise and balanced book based on personal experience; *God Among the Ruins* by Mags Duggan (BRF Ministries, 2018) describes the author's struggle with faith after a painful loss; and my own *Deep Calls to Deep* (BRF Ministries, second edition 2021) looks at some Psalms of lament along with stories of people who found themselves in difficult places.

Point of connection

It is inevitable that at some point in our journey we will experience some major turbulence and stormy weather. This often takes us by surprise, although it is to be expected. Times of testing, the experience of conflict, the pain of misunderstanding, and the shattering of our dreams are part and parcel of life. It is how we respond to setbacks and difficulties that matters. If we face hardship with God's help, and in humility learn lessons about ourselves, these stumbling blocks can become stepping stones to a stronger faith and a deeper character. This does not happen automatically, however. We must choose to receive God's grace for the situation, even if with a shaky hand.

- I describe two major points of testing in this part of my story. What can you learn from each, and from my response (whether good or bad)?

- Sometimes we must take a stand for that which we believe is right, and our soul is formed more deeply when we are willing to bear the pain of living by our convictions. When have you been called to take a stand? How did that work out for you?

- How do you understand the expression 'falling into grace'? What do you consider to be the difference between legalism, licence, and true Christian liberty?

- Can you bring to mind a time when you found yourself disappointed with God? If so, what circumstances brought that about? How did you get through that experience?

- Times of testing and disappointments may challenge how we understand the Christian life. We may naïvely think that since we are following God all will be well, and pain and hurt will not touch us. When they do, we may be thrown into turmoil and forced to rethink our faith, to move into a more mature expression of discipleship that takes suffering into account and is more comfortable with the mystery of God. Are you conscious of reframing your mental map of the Christian journey? If so, how is it changing?

On your timeline, you may like to mark any moments when your faith has been shaken, and you experienced disappointment with God.

7

SHARPENING

He made my mouth like a sharpened sword, in the shadow of his hand he hid me; he made me into a polished arrow and concealed me in his quiver.

ISAIAH 49:2

God's transforming work within us must always precede the transforming work God desires to do through us.

Randy Reese and Robert Loane[26]

It took some time for the Hemsworth congregation to re-establish itself but slowly we began to find a new identity and purpose, although the next four years were not easy. From my own perspective, I felt a greater freedom to teach the things I was learning for myself, rather than simply reproduce a narrow party line.

Finding my fit

An interesting change was happening inside me. I began to see that my main gifting was in fact teaching, with the pastoral gift alongside it, and then administration as a supporting gift. This identification of a major gift, surrounded by a cluster of supporting gifts, seems to be a normal development when it comes to recognising our spiritual gifts and how we use them. I enjoyed leading seminars and interacting with people around the material I shared, and I longed to do more of this sort of ministry. A restlessness developed inside me, and I felt it was perhaps time for a move. I had never previously chosen to leave a placement, so this was a new feeling. When I shared it with Evelyn she wisely said, 'I don't care what you do next but let it build on what you have done before.'

In the autumn of 1992, an opportunity arose at Bawtry Hall, a Christian conference centre not far away, near Doncaster, to head up the Equip training programme. This was a newish venture under the auspices of Action Partners Ministries and based at the newly refurbished hall. With an emphasis on training for mission, the role was to coordinate the programme as well as to teach some of the courses. It sounded right up my street, building on what I had done before and challenging me in new ways. I applied and was given the job, starting work in January the following year.

I found immediately that I loved being in this new environment. Released from the daily demands of pastoral leadership and surrounded by people who were mature in their faith, I felt an immediate growth spurt as a person. Bawtry Hall was run by a mission called Action Partners, whose focus was on Africa, but the hall itself was home to several other Christian organisations, so there was a real buzz about the place. Together with another staff member, Andrew Trigger, and our P.A., Barbara Jacquess, we set about building a programme of residential and day events that would meet the needs of the Action Partners staff, as well as mission partners from other organisations, and church leaders both locally and nationally.

It took time for the programme to develop and become known, but with good publicity and working hard at networking, it became established and appreciated widely. We ran orientation courses for those going overseas to work, as well as re-entry seminars for people returning and coming to an end of their work in mission. An innovative component was an annual holiday for missionary children to help them adjust to life in Britian, which was not 'home' for most of them. Then there were courses such as stress management, leadership development, presentation skills, and Myers-Briggs workshops. Often, we brought in experts to teach for us, but we taught many courses ourselves. I found myself learning so many new things and growing in my ability to teach at a new level.

A new church

Meanwhile, we had planted a new congregation from the Hemsworth church in the nearby village of Ackworth, and it was decided that I would lead that new work, while others cared for the established congregation. Little did I realise that Ackworth Community Church (ACC) would become my spiritual home for the next 30 years! We started with a small group of twelve people, meeting in a rented building, and although growth was slow, a church was born. I worked very closely with Ashley Guest, who had grown up in Hemsworth and who was eventually employed by the Ackworth church. From its inception, the church was outward looking, serving the needs of the village through a mums and toddlers group, and proclaiming the good news of Jesus as much as possible.

It is very hard to measure the impact that a church has, or to assess how close it is to the pattern God has for his church – if, indeed, he has one! God is a God of infinite variety, and I guess no two churches are the same, nor should they be. We had expected the church to grow more than it did, but given the demographics of that area (one of the lowest church-going areas in the country), perhaps it is not surprising that it has stayed quite small. Yet there can be a particular beauty in a small church, and I would say of the Ackworth church that it was 'small but beautifully formed'! There has always been an openness to God and his Spirit, a strong love for Jesus, a recognition of the importance of mission, and the priority of prayer. Some of the members have been friends and fellow disciples for many years, and the roots of fellowship and shared spiritual history run very deep. It is a safe place, where people are known and loved.

This was a period for me of growing again in confidence, of spreading my wings and finding I could fly, especially in my work at Bawtry Hall. I discovered the importance of listening well to people, and this brought my teaching and pastoral gifts together in a way that was appreciated. I found that I naturally mentored other people, and my work provided many opportunities to lend a listening ear to those in ministry who were weary and hurting. My own pain in ministry enabled me to empathise with others going through difficulties and I began to see how God had redeemed the hurt and used it to make me a deeper, more compassionate person.

Deep stirrings

I was now well into my 40s and entering the midlife period, when often without realising it, we begin to reappraise our lives. Deep questions emerge within us, often about our purpose in life, the direction we are taking, and what faith means to us. It can be either a destructive or a constructive period, depending on how we respond to the inner turmoil that happens inside us. I felt some of this inner *angst* from time to time and looked in vain for help and guidance. I didn't know then that God is characteristically at work in this form of upheaval, or that midlife is perhaps the most formative period in the spiritual life, but God knew what he was doing and where he was taking me.

During this time I was conscious of two deep currents within me calling for my attention. The first was a feeling of exhaustion that I lived with most of the time. Life was very full, with the increasing demands of the work at Bawtry Hall, and then church commitments in my 'spare' time, plus family life with its challenges. I said to myself, 'This doesn't feel like the abundant life Jesus promised. This is the exhausted life. There must be a better way to live than this.' When two of my close friends in ministry experienced burnout and needed to take time off work to recover, I realised it was a wake-up call to me as well. I needed to examine the way I was living and make adjustments.

The second stirring in my soul was a longing to know Jesus more deeply. It wasn't that my spiritual life was dried up or lacklustre, but an increasing sense that there was something more, something deeper yet to be discovered. I had come through the evangelical tradition and had a strong relationship with God that was firmly rooted in scripture. I was at home, too, in the charismatic tradition, filled with the Spirit and delighting in heart-felt worship and spiritual gifts. Yet I sensed a piece of the jigsaw was missing, but I didn't know exactly what it was.

I came across Eugene Peterson's paraphrase of Matthew 11:28–30 in *The Message*, a well-known passage often used in gospel presentations, but given a new and relevant twist in his version:

> 'Are you tired? Worn out? Burned out on religion? Come to me. Get away with me and you'll recover your life. I'll show you how to take a real rest. Walk with me and work with me – watch how I do it. Learn the unforced rhythms of grace. I won't lay anything heavy or ill-fitting on you. Keep company with me and you'll learn to live freely and lightly.'

These words were water to my soul and seemed to speak right into my situation. I saw that I needed to learn how to work *with* Jesus, not simply *for* Jesus. He was inviting me into a partnership with himself, and if I accepted his invitation (his yoke) I would discover a way of serving him that was sustainable and enjoyable, rather than exhausting. I saw too that he was calling me to spend more time with him, to get to know him more deeply by being with him. It was a call to intimacy, to closeness, to friendship. The two deep currents in my heart began to flow together, in the same direction, creating in me a longing and a yearning that could not be resisted. Simply put, it was a longing for Jesus.

Time to take stock

The year 2000 arrived without any great alarm. Our computers did not crash as predicted, the world was still turning, and there was little difference apart from the awareness that we were living in a new millennium. I had been working at the hall for seven years and asked for a sabbatical, both to rest and to explore the new direction I felt my heart was taking – into the contemplative tradition. Everything seemed to be pointing me in the direction of this third strand of healthy spirituality which I instinctively felt held the key to sustainable ministry and a greater intimacy with Jesus. In March, I turned 50 and began a three-month sabbatical, eager to see what God had to teach me but with no awareness of what major changes lay ahead of me.

Reflection 7:

THE MIDLIFE EXPERIENCE

I have already described something of my midlife journey, but I want to enlarge upon it here because of my conviction that this is often a major transition point, not only in life but in our relationship with God as well. If you have reached midlife yourself, or can now look back on it, you will probably know this for yourself.

The psalmist says, 'I was young and now I am old' (Psalm 37:25). In a few short words he sums up the life passage we are thinking about – from being young (the first half) to becoming old (the second half). In our 40s or 50s we become aware of changes taking place within us, physically, emotionally, and spiritually. These changes are often gradual, occurring maybe over a decade, but quite profound and demanding our attention. Something is happening within us, but we are not sure what, and it can feel disorientating.

For many there is a *review of the past*. This may be a nostalgic glance over our shoulder to the happier times of our youth at school or college. It may also be expressed as a need to get in touch with our past, to understand what happened back then, and to deal with the pain we experienced but never dealt with. We want to put the pieces together and make sense of them so we can have peace. It could be that it is time to appraise our past, to re-evaluate our hopes and dreams and to consider if we want to continue in the same direction or not.

For most there will be a period of necessary self-absorption as we *reassess the present*, taking time to have a good long look at our life and to understand ourselves better. By this stage, life will have thrown up some major challenges and we will have learnt things about ourselves of which we were previously unaware, not all of them positive. We may have known failure, not seen the success we expected or hoped for, and may want to adopt a more realistic assessment of our abilities. Or we may have been successful and are wondering what comes next, and whether achieving our goals has given us satisfaction.

Some searching questions may have emerged. Is this as good as it gets? Is this all there is to life? Do I have to continue like this for another 30 or 40 years? How can I get off this treadmill? Who am I really, and how can I be true to myself? Is God who I thought he was? Such questions can shake us to our foundations and may cause us to lose our way. That is why midlife is a dangerous time and explains why some people during such personal turmoil make bad decisions and take wrong turnings.

What is helpful during this time is finding someone to talk to honestly about our struggles – a counsellor, mentor, or spiritual director. There is nothing shameful about needing help to navigate midlife. Indeed, wisdom demands that we have the courage to do so. God is at work in the turmoil and seeking to draw us into a closer relationship with himself where we learn to depend more fully on him and seek his will for the next part of our life. That's why, if we open ourselves to God, midlife can be the most formative period of all.

One of the key issues during this time of struggle is to become authentic, to anchor our identity in God and in who he made us to be, rather than in some imagined version of ourself that has been forced on us by others or fashioned out of who we think others want us to be. This, of course, brings with it the realisation that our identity is given to us by God, not created by ourselves. We are his deeply loved children and, as such, have an intrinsic and lasting value simply because we belong to him. How liberating that truth can be!

Alongside this, it is during midlife that we realise we cannot live at the pace we used to, and that natural strength is both limited and inadequate to sustain a life of service to God. This may find its expression in a full-blown burnout, or in a general sense of realisation that the way we are living is unsustainable. This in turn forces us back to God, to experience what some have called 'the divine exchange', when having come to the end of our own resources, we begin to learn how to allow God to live in us and through us. These two major lessons both normally occur within the midlife transition and are vital factors in our fruitfulness as we go forward into the second half of life.

The *angst* of midlife comes and goes but the transition itself may take several years, even a decade. Part of the process will be to chart our course for the second half of life, hopefully finding a match between our personality, gifting, and the call of God. This may mean continuing what we are already doing, but in greater dependency on God and with less exhausting self-effort. Often it may mean moving in a different direction altogether, and under the guidance of God taking bold steps of faith into a new adventure with him. What we are looking for now is our God-given vocation. This is beautifully summed up in the words of writer Frederick Buechner: 'The place God calls you to is the place where your deep gladness and the world's deep hunger meet.'[27] This is the sweet spot where we find ourselves doing that for which we were made. It is where we are most efficient and most effective, and hopefully is the outcome of a well-navigated midlife journey.

As you continue to read my story, what you will notice is that for me, my sabbatical (aged 50) became a crossing place where, after a long period of inner change, I came out of the midlife phase and entered the second half of my life. Looking back, it was like traversing a river, leaving one country to emerge again on the other side in a new one. I did so with a renewed sense of calling, to establish my own ministry and to help others into contemplative spirituality. More than that, I had a stronger sense of my identity as God's deeply loved child and had been released from some of the emotional insecurities that had plagued me in the first half of my life. I was also learning how to work in partnership with God in a way that would mean the demands of later years would be sustainable.

Point of connection

Almost all writers about leadership development and spiritual formation agree on one thing – that midlife, whenever it occurs, is a crucial time for us. I have no doubt about this myself, from my own experience, and from my observation of others at this stage. Some readers may not yet have reached their 40s and 50s, but it is still helpful to be informed about what may lie ahead. Others may be in the thick of it, and keen to learn. Some may be looking back wistfully over their shoulders to a different era, but happy to reflect on the events of those days.

- What do you feel about the emergence in time of a main gift out of the cluster of gifts that God has given you? Are you able to identify your personal gifts? Do you know how they work together? And do you feel that you too have a dominant gift? Identifying it may shape the course of future ministry.

- How do we know when it is time to move on from a particular role or calling? Sometimes it is necessary to move so that we can grow further, and our gifts find a new expression. As you look back, what has caused you to move on in ministry? How did you know it was God's will?

- Do you identify with the 'stirrings' I experienced within me as I approached midlife? What about the two deep currents – to find a way to serve passionately without burning out, and to know Jesus more deeply? Do they resonate with you? What other currents may be stirring in you?

- As you read the reflection on midlife, from whatever standpoint (before, during, after), what are your thoughts and feelings? Is this period as important as I, and others, suggest? What is going on during midlife, and how is God at work in us during this life transition?

- Several times we read about the wisdom of having a mentor, spiritual director, counsellor, and so on. Would this be helpful for you if it is not already in place?

On your timeline you may wish to identify your midlife period. It could be anywhere from 40 to 60 years. Reflect on this period in the light of what you have been reading.

8

DEEPENING

'Be still, and know that I am God; I will be exalted among the nations, I will be exalted in the earth.'
PSALM 46:10

Superficiality is the curse of our age. The doctrine of instant sanctification is a primary problem. The desperate need today is not for a greater number of intelligent people, or gifted people, but for deep people.
Richard Foster[28]

My sabbatical began as planned but coincided with some rather long and drawn-out improvements to our bathroom at home which were both noisy and stressful. Not exactly the beginning I had expected, but that's real life, isn't it? I appreciated time to read around the subject of contemplative spirituality, being greatly helped by Alexander Ryrie's book, *Silent Waiting* (Canterbury Press, 1999) which explores the biblical roots of contemplative spirituality and was exactly what I needed given my evangelical background.

I also talked to those already in the contemplative stream and visited the Northumbria Community to find out more. I had recently been introduced to their worship songs, which I loved, and their Celtic daily prayer. This was the first time I had encountered Christ-centred, Spirit-filled liturgy, and it moved me deeply, creating in me a hunger for more. The main event in my sabbatical diary, however, was to be a five-day retreat with David and Joyce Huggett at their home in Derbyshire.

Stepping aside

I first met the Huggetts at Bawtry Hall when they came to teach some sessions on self-care for those in mission. David had been vicar of a thriving church in Nottingham and Joyce a well-known writer before they moved out to Cyprus to hold retreats for missionaries. On their return they had established a similar centre in Derbyshire and when they heard I was taking a sabbatical, they invited me to go and have a personal retreat with them. It had seemed like a good idea at the time, but as the moment drew near, I became quite apprehensive, never having been on a retreat before, but also wondering how I would cope with five days without TV or a newspaper, and in my own company. Again, Evelyn's practical wisdom was applied. 'Well, if you don't like it, you can always come home,' she said in her understated way.

I duly arrived at their place and was warmly greeted by Joyce who would lead me through my retreat. Having shown me my room, she then took me to a small lounge, which would be mine to use during the retreat, and left me to it until our first session the next morning. I sat in the stillness, enjoying the beautiful view of the Derbyshire hills, and felt such a peace come over me. I had never encountered true silence before, and it seemed as if God was there to greet me as well, welcoming me into his presence. My soul was so in need, not just of rest, but of stillness and silence, and I could feel my spirit respond to this moment.

During the next few days, I met regularly with Joyce, and she helped me get in touch with my inner life, and to hear the still, small voice of God. She asked me to spend time meditating on John 15 in *The Message* version, in particular what Jesus says about the vine and the branches. I was familiar with these verses and had experienced God's pruning work already in my life, but now I saw something new, an invitation from Jesus that I could not resist: 'Live in me. Make your home in me just as I do in you' (v. 4). As I read on, I then saw the key to everything: 'I am the Vine, you are the branches. When you're joined with me and I with you, the relation intimate and organic, the harvest is sure to be abundant' (v. 5).

Intimate and organic. I was being invited into a loving relationship with Jesus where he would live his life in me and through me, and then quite naturally and without striving or straining, my life would become fruitful for his glory. This truth is at the heart of contemplative spirituality, and it is a revolutionary insight for those who have tried their very best, in their own strength, to make things happen for God.

I had many questions to ask Joyce, and much of the week was spent learning more about contemplation and how to practically abide in Christ. I had become so alive in Christ it seemed like a second conversion, as if I had been 'baptised into silence'. It was the start of a new journey for me, and for the rest of my sabbatical I continued to read and to write up my findings.

I returned refreshed to Bawtry Hall and determined to introduce retreats and Quiet Days to the Equip programme. Joyce came to lead a retreat and continued to mentor me as I sought to integrate the three strands together – evangelical, charismatic, and contemplative. As my understanding grew, and with encouragement from Joyce, I began to lead Quiet Days and eventually retreats.

Finding my true identity

So much seemed to be happening within me as I opened myself up to God and sought a new level of intimacy with him. I knew there were some issues inside me that needed sorting before this could happen more fully, and on a later retreat with Joyce, I was able to let them surface and be dealt with. I began to discover my true identity as God's deeply loved child, something I had only known in theory before. I devoured books like *Return of the Prodigal* by Henri Nouwen (DLT, 1994) and *Abba's Child* by Brennan Manning (Nav Press, 1994), and their insights helped to bring further healing to some of my attachment issues from childhood. I became more content with my own company and less disturbed by being alone. All of this was an extension of the message of grace that was already so precious to me and is summed up beautifully in the words of John Eagan, quoted by Brennan Manning: 'Define yourself radically as one beloved by God. This is the true self. Every other identity is an illusion.'[29]

I continued to work on the write-up of my sabbatical exploration of contemplative spirituality and with Joyce's help, to polish the manuscript. I gave it a title, 'The call to intimacy', as I felt this was indeed something the Spirit was saying to the church in general. She encouraged me to send it to a publisher, which I did, but it was rejected. I guess I was an 'unknown' and they didn't want to take a risk with me, but it was disappointing. Most writers know the pain of rejection, and it is perhaps good to have knocks like this, so we sharpen our skills and learn how to improve our writing. Joyce encouraged me to persevere and said she knew a bookseller in Singapore who was looking to move into publishing. I sent him the manuscript, and to my amazement, he was willing to publish it. That was an exciting moment, and I waited expectantly for the day the first copy would arrive.

Time for change

One of the developments at Bawtry Hall was a joint initiative with Mission Aviation Fellowship (MAF) to run a three-week orientation programme designed for their own personnel, but open to others from any smaller missions without the resources to run such a course. Called 'Preparing for change', this course ran several times, and I forged strong links with MAF which would later become very significant. I also trained to be a Myers-Briggs practitioner and ran many courses at the hall to help those attending to better understand themselves and others. This approach to identifying and understanding personality preferences has many different applications, and I especially enjoyed helping people apply their learning to the spiritual life and in leadership situations.

After almost ten years at the hall, I began to sense it was time to move on but was taken by surprise by what the Lord had in mind. I was on retreat again in Derbyshire with the Huggetts, and during my stay had a tremendous sense that it was time to step out of the familiar and into the unknown. I felt God saying I should focus more on retreats and mentoring individuals, and that this would require me to start my own ministry. This came as quite a shock and I remember the tears flowed as I considered what it would mean letting go of – a stable job with a steady income, and the security and status it gave me. I also wondered how Evelyn would respond.

We took our time to think about it, but both concluded that this was from God. It was the first time I experienced God speaking to me directly through a dream, and it happened twice. On the first occasion, my hand was open, and a small bird flew into my palm. I assumed it had come so I could feed it, but it flew away again and then returned, placing a small piece of bread in my hand. As I woke, I felt God say he would provide for all our needs.

On the second occasion, I was in a foreign land and noticing ladies in brightly coloured dresses sitting by the roadside selling fruits which I didn't recognise. When I asked what the fruits were, they replied in a language I didn't understand. When I woke, I felt God say, 'You will bear fruit of a kind you have never borne before.' Both dreams were vivid, and memorable, and the message they contained became true in our experience – God met our needs financially and my ministry took a new direction. They were not the basis of our decision, but they gave confirmation to what we were already sensing was from God and injected a necessary measure of faith into our plans.

I was sad to leave Bawtry Hall and the friends I had made there, but I knew God was calling me to move on into a new phase of ministry.

So, in July 2002, I launched out and began in freelance ministry. God was inviting us again to follow his leading, and it was scary, but once more we would experience his faithfulness and see doors of opportunity open that we could never have imagined or expected. Wherever he leads we must follow.

Reflection 8:

FAITH GROWING AND DEVELOPING

Faith is the word that best describes our part in the relationship we have with God, how we respond to his overture of grace and receive all he wants to give us. We choose to believe *in* him, not simply by giving mental assent to certain doctrines or creeds, but by placing our trust in him for our future and acting accordingly. We believe that he is there, that he is good, and has a purpose for our lives to which we give ourselves fully. That is faith, and without such faith it is not possible to please God (Hebrews 11:6).

Faith connects us to God. Grace offers to us the gift of salvation, and faith takes hold of it by believing the offer is real and genuine and is available to us personally. Hence Paul famously writes, 'For it is by grace you have been saved, through faith – and this is not from your-selves, it is the gift of God – not by works, so that no-one can boast' (Ephesians 2:8–9). By grace and through faith; God's part followed by our part. The Christian life always operates in this way. God gives, and we receive.

The Christian life is a life of faith, beautifully illustrated for us in Hebrews 11, a chapter filled with the stories of men and women who chose to live their lives 'by faith' (as the writer frequently says), whether in success or failure, triumph or tragedy. As we, too, learn to live by faith, our story joins with their stories and becomes part of the greater story of God.

When we first come to faith – that is, place our trust in Jesus (John 1:12) – our faith is simple, clear, and uncomplicated. We take God at his word, become part of the church, seek to live our lives for his glory, and get on with the business of being a disciple. This may be the pattern for many years as we learn the great doctrines of the faith and model our life as best we can on the life of Jesus. But faith develops and changes over time. It is dynamic and its form and expression evolve as we continue to follow Jesus. While some may choose to stay in what we may call the 'simple faith' stage, others find their faith is changing. They become restless, discontented, and feel the need to push back the boundaries of their faith.

This can be a painful time for them, and their friends, as they begin to question some long-cherished beliefs and practices, but these are growing pains and to be expected in healthy spiritual development. Sometimes intellectual questions arise. Is the Bible reliable? Why does God allow evil? Why is there so much violence in the Old Testament? Occasionally this questioning is prompted by personal experiences that create doubt and confusion. Why are my prayers not answered? Why didn't God heal my friend? Why are church leaders guilty of abuse, and churches so unwelcoming? Why do I feel disappointed with God? Often the culture we live in forces us to ask serious questions. What is God's attitude towards homosexuality? What does God think about abortion and euthanasia? Is the teaching of the church still relevant?

At times this can feel disconcerting and disorientating as we lose our bearings and certainty seems to evaporate. Often people have said to me, 'I think I am losing my faith.' My answer is always, 'Perhaps you are finding it,' because what is happening is that our faith is being reformed and reshaped. It is growing and maturing. We are in fact finding it for ourselves, and it is God's Spirit who is behind our questioning and searching, leading us to a deeper, richer expression of faith.

This cross-examining of our faith often occurs during the midlife period, when a lot of other things are changing within us, but it is part of developing a more grown-up faith. We must develop personal convictions and come to know what we believe, not simply what other people (and churches) tell us we should believe. This is a good time to seek out a mentor or spiritual director, someone who can provide a safe place for us to explore our doubts and fears, and yet gently help us to stay in touch with God. Without such help people can easily lose their way and drop out of church altogether.

Eventually the period of turmoil subsides somewhat, and hopefully we come out the other side with our faith still intact but changed. We know what aspects of our faith really matter to us, and what is of secondary importance. We realise we can't understand everything but are content to live with mystery and ambiguity. In short, we are less certain about some things, but surer of others – for instance, of the reality of God and his grip of grace upon our lives. Our confidence is now less built around dogma but more fully centred on God himself. We live now on the basis of faith expressed through our trust in a faithful God. This is a more mature faith which will continue to deepen and develop, albeit maybe less dramatically.

New Zealand Baptist minister Alan Jamieson has researched this transformation in the faith journey and likens it to the way a caterpillar becomes a chrysalis and then morphs into a beautiful butterfly. He writes, 'Our journey of Christian faith is a whole of life experience. It is an epic journey: more an ultramarathon than a quick sprint. Because it is a marathon, it is not all the same. For each of us faith changes and develops.'[30] He suggests a threefold movement from the certainties of a pre-critical phase, into the confusion of a hyper-critical phase, before arriving at a more settled post-critical phase. This is, of course, a dangerous journey which some choose not to make, while others lose their way; but for those who persevere it leads to a richer, deeper faith.

If I look at my own inner journey, I can see this process being worked out but would use more positive terminology – a movement from certainty to searching and on to intimacy. I can also express it in another way.

To begin with *I was taught* about the Christian faith, through my time as a new believer in the Methodist Church to my time at Bible college. I learned the fundamentals of the faith and believed the things I was taught.

Then *I taught others* what I had been taught, especially during my time in Malaysia.

After we returned to England, the difficulties I went through, both with the mission and in my local church context, caused me to enter a time of re-evaluation and adjustment. I began to recognise the message God had uniquely given to me to share with others, that of intimacy with God through the experience of grace.

Eventually I began to *teach others that which I had come to understand* myself, the truth which I know now with most certainty. It is not the whole truth, but one aspect of God's truth of which I am most convinced myself and can share most effectively. This is where I am now.

I would not want to suggest that we reach a point where we have arrived, and we stop growing in our faith. Our faith continues to develop and mature. We remain open to what the Spirit is teaching us, and to new ways in which he may be at work in us. We say with the apostle Paul, 'Not that I have already obtained all this, or have already arrived at my goal, but I press on to take hold of that for which Christ Jesus took hold of me' (Philippians 3:12).

Point of connection

The post-midlife period is often a time when we are internalising the changes that have been taking place within us and preparing ourselves for a new thrust into the second half of life. It feels almost as if we are learning to walk again, and it is appropriate to go slowly for a while until we get the hang of how we are to live in the second half of life.

- The narrative describes how I was impacted by the spiritual discipline of retreat – taking time away to be still and quiet and reflect on life in the company of an experienced guide. How familiar are you with this practice? If retreat is part of your normal rhythm, how does it help you? If not, are you open to explore this helpful practice? How might you begin?

- Why not meditate on John 15:1–8 in *The Message* version. What does God say to you?

- Have you ever taken a sabbatical? If so, how did that work out for you, and what was its value?

- One of the outcomes of sabbatical time for me was the discovery of my identity as God's deeply loved child. Is that something you have become aware of for yourself? What difference might it make to have this truth as the bedrock of your identity?

- If you have reached midlife already, have you noticed any changes in your own expression of faith? Has there been any time of disorientation, questioning, or searching? Where are you at right now?

- How do you think the church can best help people whose faith is undergoing a transformation?

On your timeline, perhaps identify key moments and events in your 50s (if you have got that far!).

9

BROADENING

Whoever believes in me, as scripture has said, rivers of living water will flow from within them.

JOHN 7:38

A fruit-bearing tree lives not for itself, but wholly for those to whom its fruit brings refreshment and life.

Andrew Murray[31]

I decided to call my new ministry Charis Training. *Charis* is the Greek word for grace, and my strapline was this: Intimacy with God through the experience of grace. This became my watchword, and everything I chose to do would need to be in line with this purpose. A wise friend asked me, 'Tony, do you think this is your life message?' That had never occurred to me, but as I pondered his question it seemed clear to me that it was – the summary of what God had uniquely formed in me and given me to share with others.

Launching out

The new ministry had two parts to it – the local (based in the Ackworth church) and the national and international. For the first time I would receive some small financial support from my local church in return for the leadership I gave them, although I never took the term 'pastor'. This would then be subsidised by what I could earn as a freelance trainer. Evelyn also was working as a nurse in local care homes, and although at times it was a precarious existence, God provided for us, and we were never lacking for anything.

At first, I wondered if anyone would know about what I was doing now I was on my own, and whether the phone would ring with an invitation to provide some training or lead a retreat, but slowly it did and I found there was plenty to do. Myers-Briggs courses provided my 'bread and butter' income, and I continued to derive great satisfaction from helping people come to understand themselves better. I have always believed that growing in self-awareness is crucial for anyone in leadership or ministry, and there was a steady demand for me to lead training events like this in a variety of settings.

Doors open

God opened doors of opportunity for me in many surprising ways. Andrew Wooding-Jones had been a vicar in Sheffield, and we had met at Bawtry Hall. When he moved down to Sussex to become director of Ashburnham Place, a large and popular conference centre south of London, he invited me to lead courses and retreats there, which I did two or three times a year for many years. Ashburnham is a beautiful place, with large, wooded grounds, and two magnificent lakes. The first retreat I did there had only seven guests, but we persevered, and over time numbers grew. Many people came back time and again, and it was great to see them grow in their faith and confidence in God, as well as become something of a supportive community to each other over the years.

MAF contacted me because they had decided to move their orientation courses nearer to their home base in Kent and wanted me to take part. This I was delighted to do, and I formed an effective partnership with Arne Nordhal, a Norwegian member of the MAF Europe board who was also a trainer. For a time, these were held at Ashburnham, then later near MAF's headquarters in Ashford. All of this meant a great deal of motorway travel and time away from home, but we regarded it as a necessary part of the new ministry life. Fortunately, I enjoy driving, and the long journeys gave me time to either prepare myself for the work ahead or unwind when it was finished.

Back to Singapore

After *The Call to Intimacy* was published in Singapore in 2001, Alan Chew, the publisher, invited me to visit and introduce the book by speaking in different churches. I found that there was a great hunger for the message of intimacy with God through the experience of grace. Most churches in Singapore are thriving, with modern buildings, growing congregations, and large staff teams, but are very driven in their approach to the Christian life and service. This means there are a lot of exhausted leaders and weary church members. The message that it is permissible to slow down, to rest, and spend time with God came as such a relief to many, and I found myself invited back time and again to teach more about the contemplative tradition.

The book itself was littered with mistakes and typos, and the formatting was often wrong, but there was something powerful about that little book which meant it spoke deeply to people. One lady, a senior leader in her mission organisation in the USA, somehow came across it while on retreat in England. She wrote to me, saying, 'The book made me realise how hungry I was for God... I didn't even realise how starved I was for something other than what I thought it was to be a Christian. For the first time in many years I felt I could breathe and relax in God's company.' A British publisher got hold of it, too, and published a new edition (minus the mistakes) under the title of *Rhythms of Grace* (Kingsway, 2004). It has been in print ever since, now published by BRF Ministries (new edition in 2025).

Alan Chew also published for me two small booklets with a music CD attached to each. The first was based on Zephaniah 3:17 and was called *The Father's Song*, describing the love God has for us as the foundation for our true identity. It sold really well and one church in Singapore gave a copy to each of its members – all 750 of them! It also proved popular with counsellors as a devotional tool to help people discover and experience the love of God for themselves. The second one, *The Shepherd's Song*, was based on Psalm 23, and again proved helpful in introducing people to the grace of God.

Writing

My fledgling writing career was gaining momentum, and when I was invited to write something for BRF Ministries, I chose to use the material which I had developed on Psalm 23. Published in 2004, the book was called *Song of the Shepherd*, and the subtitle accurately describes what it is about – 'Meeting the God of grace in Psalm 23'. It is a very familiar psalm, but I was seeing it through new eyes after my own discovery of grace and the unconditional love of God. The structure was very simple: once we have a relationship with the good shepherd, we can learn to rest, then learn to trust, and finally learn to live. Strangely, even though it has such an encouraging message, it is the only one of my books no longer in print.

Penhurst

While at Bawtry Hall I had been asked to give some advice to a group of people who were opening a new retreat centre in Sussex, based in a 17th-century manor house in the hamlet of Penhurst. The house had been the home of Paul Broomhall and his family, himself a lifelong supporter of overseas mission and a distant relative of Hudson Taylor. Their vision was to use the house as a welcoming space for missionaries, and soon after it opened in 2002, I was invited to lead one of the first retreats. I immediately felt at home there, and have been leading retreats there ever since, right up until the present time. It is one of those places where, with its quiet location, gracious furnishings, and warm welcome, it is easy to encounter God.

Heart cries – finding rest

My new ministry was going well, but this period (2002–5) was far from easy in the church part of my life. I had started to journal when I first went on retreat with Joyce Huggett and continued the discipline but mostly when I was under pressure and needing God's help. As I have re-read my entries for this period, two themes emerge constantly – my feeling of exhaustion and many heartfelt cries to God for his intervention in the leadership challenges we were facing at Ackworth.

On one of my trips to Singapore, as I returned in the evening to my hotel utterly worn out, I sensed God say to me, 'Tony, unless you learn to rest in me, you will never survive in freelance ministry.' I had clearly not yet discovered how to work in partnership with God and was striving to make things happen. Through my exploration of the contemplative tradition, I had begun to see the importance of the gift of sabbath, a day of rest in the midst of a busy week. What I had not yet realised was that sabbath is meant to be a way of life, not a pause in a busy schedule. My natural response was to work hard, give of my best, and take the responsibility on my own shoulders. Something had to change. I needed to find God's rest.

Many of God's major lessons take root in us slowly, and it was only gradually – and after much failing – that I began to learn how to work from a place of rest. I was helped in my understanding by Marva Dawn's wonderful book, *Keeping the Sabbath Wholly* (Eerdmans, 2001) where she develops the thought of sabbath as rest – spiritually, physically, emotionally, intellectually, and socially. She writes, 'To rest utterly in the grace of God is the foundation for wholistic rest.'[32] Then she quotes Eugene Peterson's explanation of the rhythm of grace, where God's activity is always previous and primary and is illustrated in the Hebrew concept of a day as evening leading to morning. 'Evening: God begins, without our help, his creative day. Morning: God calls us to enjoy and share and develop the work he initiated.'[33]

I began to see that this leads to a different way of working. We do not work *into* rest, as if it were a reward for hard work, but *from* a place of rest, trusting that it is God's work, and he will accomplish his purpose through us. We do not need to strive or strain but simply cooperate with his working in us. We are not simply passive, but responsive to his leading and guiding, listening for the prompting of his Spirit. It all boils down to dependency and letting go of our independent patterns of behaviour. For many of us, this will require a degree of brokenness first, of recognising that we cannot do the work of God in our own strength.

Heart cries – finding strength

At the same time as I was learning this key lesson, I was struggling with some serious issues within the Ackworth church. We had a difficult and sensitive pastoral situation to deal with, which dragged on and on, and gave me many sleepless nights. Then, one of our elders (who was also my closest friend) suddenly resigned and left the church. It was a devastating blow, and these two situations combined to rock both me and the church. I experienced what I described in my journal as 'free-floating anxiety', a state of continual dis-ease. I had a sense that this was a test of my ability as a leader – did I have what it takes to steer the ship through these stormy seas? I was not at all convinced I had.

As I read again my journals, I can see not only my pain but how God brought me (and the church) through this period. My sense of weakness caused me to cry out to God for his help, and my brokenness was his way of creating a deeper dependency in me. I see that he spoke to me many times from his word, with encouragement, comfort, and the strength to continue. There were also many 'sweet comforts' along the way, those little indications of God's presence and blessing even during confusion and hurt. All I could do was to surrender myself to God. Perhaps that was what he most wanted anyway?

One of the things that sustained me during this turmoil was a regular Quiet Day with a small group of trusted friends, including Jonathan Dunning and Baz Gascoigne, two church leaders from Sheffield, and my dear friend Ashley Guest. They formed the core of a group of us who met bimonthly at Hexthorpe Manor, a retreat house in Doncaster. Those days were life-giving to me; lots of fun and laughter, honest sharing and supportive listening, and a rich experience of God as we shared our thoughts based on Richard Foster's book, *Streams of Living Water* (Harper Collins, 1998). And of course, prayer and worship. This group continued to meet in different venues over the next 20 years, and for me was an oasis, one of the places where my soul was refreshed and renewed time and again.

It was on a return visit to Bawtry Hall, though, that the turning point came, and God spoke to me clearly about the church situation. It was a grey, damp, November day, and in the lunch break I went out for a walk. My soul was troubled, but as I walked the words of a hymn floated unbidden into my mind: 'Bright skies will soon be o'er me, Where the dark clouds have been.'[34] Then, as I turned the corner, I saw before me a local landmark, the Turkey Oaks – two majestic oak trees standing tall and erect, but their branches stripped of leaves. I felt God say to me, 'They are bare now, but they won't always be.' It was his word of hope to my soul, and my spirit leapt within me. Yes, as sure as spring will come and the trees will bud again, so the Ackworth church would survive this wintering period.

It did not happen magically or immediately, but we did turn the corner. At one leadership meeting in particular there was reconciliation and a renewal of our commitment to the church. Trust was rekindled, and we found grace to move forward again together. In the coldness of the winter season our roots had gone deeper, and we were stronger for the testing.

Another step of faith

With a renewed stability in the church, we decided to call a full-time pastor, and appointed Brian Donner in 2005. Brian came from a background in business but had been active in church leadership all his life. Having recently retired he wanted to give some time to Christian ministry, and he and his wife Linda seemed a perfect match for the church. They were able to relocate to Ackworth, and soon settled in the village, forming many new contacts and introducing the Alpha course.

Their arrival freed me to focus fully on my own ministry, so we decided to sell our family home, which was too large anyway now the children had left, pay off our mortgage, buy a small bungalow, and use the surplus cash to support ourselves going forward. I remember crying when I saw the 'For sale' sign go up outside the house, our home for 21 years, which we had loved dearly, and which had been God's gift to us when we had returned from Malaysia. It was the right thing to do, however, and released us to take another big step of faith and embrace fully the new season into which God was calling us.

Reflection 9:

INVITATION TO TRANSFORMATION

Following Jesus is not just about doing things for God but becoming like him. Jesus called the first disciples with a clear goal in mind – 'that they might be with him, and that he might send them out to preach' (Mark 3:14). Notice that the priority was for them to be with him, learning from him, absorbing his teaching, and then, by implication, to become like him. Discipleship is first about being and becoming, and then doing – in this case being sent out in mission. The two are equally important, but the transformation of life provides the foundation for effective ministry in the world.

The process by which we become more like Christ is called spiritual formation, an expression which I have come to love as it encapsulates the work God is doing in us as we go through life and even as we are busily serving him. Our becoming like Christ is the great desire of the Father for each of his children, the purpose behind all other purposes. Spiritual formation is the process by which this happens – the way we are being changed into the likeness of Christ in our thoughts, words, and actions, and by which we are being made increasingly fruitful in our service for God.

There is a clear biblical framework for this interior, often hidden, work of God with which we are called to cooperate. Paul gives expression to it in several places. It seems to have been his passion in ministry.

To the Galatians he writes, 'My dear children, for whom I am again in the pains of childbirth until Christ is formed in you' (Galatians 4:19). Here we see that transformation does not happen easily. Believers are often resistant to change, and it can be hard work for those who seek to help them grow in Christ, but the *goal* is clear – become like Jesus. Change takes time, and is a long, slow work that requires perseverance.

Then again, Paul says to the church in Rome, 'For those God foreknew he also predestined to be conformed to the image of his Son, that he might be the firstborn among many brothers and sisters' (Romans 8:29). *The Message* helpfully paraphrases this verse as 'God knew what he was doing from the very beginning. He decided from the outset to shape the lives of those who love him along the same lines as the life of his Son.' Here we see there is a definite *pattern* in mind, which pre-dates our conversion and even creation itself. This is what the Father has always had in mind for his children, that they should be like him and bear the family likeness. Jesus, the Son, perfectly models this, the prototype of many who will also reflect the image of God.

Finally, Paul writes, 'Do not conform to the pattern of this world, but be transformed by the renewing of your mind' (Romans 12:2). Here is the *challenge*. If we are being shaped and formed into a particular like-ness, the image of Christ, then by implication, we are not to follow the ways of the society around us, with its pressure to live, think, and act in certain ways. Rather, we are to be countercultural and be moulded into the ways of Christ and of his kingdom. The key to this lies in our way of thinking. Our thoughts must be changed so that we think like Christ. Our minds must be renewed, being set free from the thought patterns we inherit from the culture in which we live and adjusted so that we think like Jesus and have God's perspective on life. In short, to have the mind of Christ.

Formed, conformed, and transformed. This is the process of shaping and moulding that is continually at work in us by the action of God, and it lasts for a lifetime. Sometimes we make rapid progress, at other times change is slow and painful, but always God is at work in us to realise this goal.

Like a potter, he is gently forming us, squeezing us into the shape he wants us to be (see Jeremiah 18:1-6).

Like the vine dresser, he knows when we need to be pruned so that we can bear more fruit (see John 15:1-8).

Like a goldsmith, he is not afraid to refine us, turning up the heat so that the dross in our lives is removed, enabling us to better reflect his glory (see Malachi 3:2-4).

Like a father, he is strong enough to discipline us when we go astray, training us through hardships so that we learn to choose the right path (see Hebrews 12:5-11).

Becoming like Christ is clearly God's design for each of us. How then does this process of change take place? The initiative is always with God, but we cooperate through our faith and obedience and intentionally choose transformation. There is a downward movement (God to us) and an upward movement (us to God).

Downward: what God does

Father, Son, and Holy Spirit are all involved in the process of transformation, but it is the Spirit in particular who is the *agent of change*. He lives within us and produces in us the lovely fruit of the Spirit, expressions of the life of Christ – love, joy, peace, patience, kindness, goodness, faithfulness, gentleness, and self-control (Galatians 5:22-23). Without his presence we would not have the power to change, and without his influence we would not desire it, either. When we are going astray, he convicts us of our sin and moves us to repentance and turning back again to the way of Christ. As we learn to recognise his voice, and to discern his movement within us and respond in obedience, he gently schools us into the ways of Christ.

God has given us the Bible so that we can know his will, and scripture is the *basis of change*. Through the gospels we are given a portrait of Jesus so we can see what he is like, and through the epistles we realise the power that is at work within us for transformation because Christ now lives within us. As we read the Bible regularly and listen to it being expounded, the Holy Spirit reveals its truth to us. The more we absorb scripture, the more our mind is changed and renewed so that we think like God and gain his perspective on life. We are enabled to discern his purpose for our lives and his will in daily living.

God then uses the circumstances of our lives to mould and shape us. This is the *context of change* – trials and tribulations can humble us and make us more dependent on him. They weaken our natural independent self and through our brokenness cause us to seek God's help. They create in us the gentleness and lowliness that character-ised Jesus. Without some form of suffering or hardship we may not be motivated towards deep or lasting change.

Upward: what we do in response

We must remember that hunger for God is a gift, and so we should be asking God for the grace to seek him with all our hearts. That said, we can place ourselves in the way of grace firstly through reflection and self-awareness. This is *the method of change*. God has given us the ability to consider our ways, and with the help of the Spirit to examine our hearts. David, the man after God's own heart, was also conscious of his weakness and in humility cries sincerely to God, 'Search me, God, and know my heart; test me and know my anxious thoughts. See if there is any offensive way in me, and lead me in the way everlasting' (Psalm 139:23–24). Self-examination is not introspection, which is self-focused in a morbid and negative way. When we examine our hearts before God, we are inviting the Holy Spirit to show us any unhelpful behaviour we may not be aware of, any sin that may be hidden from us, and then to help us to change. Keeping a clear conscience is integral to this desire for holiness.

Added to this, we can make use of spiritual disciplines, or holy habits, those practices which help us to connect with God and maintain our abiding in Christ. These are the *means of change*. The discipline of regular Bible reading, prayer, worship, fellowship with others, serving our community, fasting, and generosity are just some of the ways we can be with God and share his love with others. In the early days of the church in Jerusalem, we read that they 'devoted themselves to the apostles' teaching and to fellowship, to the breaking of bread and to prayer' (Acts 2:42). We should not do these things as an obligation (something we must do) as that will become burdensome, but because we desire to grow in our faith. Neither should we do them to gain God's favour or impress him (there is no need), but because we want to express our love for him.

Furthermore, we can meet regularly with other disciples who are passionate for God, both our church community and perhaps a small group of individuals who are also seeking to become more like Christ. Such people are the *inspiration for change*. We are not meant to live the Christian life in isolation but in partnership with others. With a group of trusted friends we can be open and vulnerable in a place of safety, love, and acceptance. We can receive both encouragement and helpful feedback that will enhance our spiritual growth. Intentionally meeting with others for the purpose of growing in Christ is essential: 'And let us consider how we may spur one another on towards love and good deeds, not giving up meeting together, as some are in the habit of doing, but encouraging one another – and all the more as you see the Day approaching' (Hebrews 10:24–25).

Over the years I have been very conscious that God's agenda for my life is not just about what I do, but who I am, and who I am becoming. I can see clearly the ways in which he has been drawing me to himself to become more like Jesus. I have felt, and still feel, a great hunger to respond to that invitation to transformation and have sought (sometimes imperfectly and inconsistently) to do my part and place myself in the way of grace. I am still, of course, a work in progress, but aware that one day we shall see him as he is, and then finally, we shall at last be fully like him (1 John 3:2).

Point of connection

Once we are on the other side of the midlife transition, we typically enter a period of renewed activity. Building on the vitality of a rejuvenated inner life, we give ourselves wholeheartedly to the call of God as we now understand it, for the second half of life. Our struggles have hopefully led us to discover the importance of abiding in Christ (like a branch in the vine, John 15:5) which is the key to fruitfulness. We are now able to work with a sense of vocation, when who we are and what we do converge, and we enjoy a feeling that 'this is what I was made for'.

- As you read my story during this period, can you identify the doors of opportunity that God opened for me to birth the new ministry? This is so often how God works. What doors are opening for you? Are any closing?

- I mention two heart cries that surfaced within me at this time. What were they, and have you experienced anything similar? What are your heart cries?

- What do you understand from what you read in the narrative about what it means to work from a place of rest? There will be more about this in the next chapter, but we see here that God was already at work in me to show me my need of working in a different way. Does this resonate with you?

- In what way might exhaustion, or burnout, be a message from God?

- Leadership at any level is a very demanding calling, and we often feel inadequate for the task. How did God meet my need for strength? How has he met that need in your situation when you have been hard pressed?

- How do you understand and practise sabbath?

- What do you understand to be the principles behind spiritual formation as highlighted in the reflection? What is God's part? How do we cooperate?

- Consider these questions in light of your own experience: how is God forming the life of Christ within you? And how are you responding to his invitation to transformation?

Perhaps on your timeline mark any key moments and events during your 60s (if you have got that far!).

10

INFLUENCING

But thanks be to God, who always leads us as captives in Christ's triumphal procession and uses us to spread the aroma of the knowledge of him everywhere.

2 CORINTHIANS 2:14

If there is any focus that the Christian leader of the future will need, it is the discipline of dwelling in the presence of One who keeps asking us, 'Do you love me? Do you love me? Do you love me?'

Henri Nouwen[35]

The next phase of my life, which covered some 13 years (2005–18), was the busiest and most significant of my whole ministry, as well as the most demanding in terms of responding to the opportunities God gave to me. These later years are, according to leadership theory, the productive years, when we are working most efficiently and effectively because we know who we are, what God has called us to do, and how to work in partnership with him. I prefer to call them the fruitful years, because all that happens is a result of abiding in Christ.

Bearing fruit

This period is also described as 'the journey outward'[36] when, after the time of inwardness associated with midlife, we focus outwards, operating now out of a sense of fullness, of being loved by God, and therefore able to love others freely. 'It is such a natural process,' say Janet Hagberg and Robert Guelich, 'that we hardly recognise it is happening.'[37] Certainly, the old striving to achieve is hopefully being replaced by a restful sense of dependency on God, allowing him to work through us and remembering that it is his work, not ours. When this happens, we seem to accomplish more with less effort as we live in the power of the Spirit.

At this time I was beginning to recognise that my own leadership was more about influencing[38] other people into the ways of God rather than leading groups of people to accomplish God-given goals and strategic visions. I am more concerned with helping individuals grow in God rather than with achieving organisational objectives. In short, I am an influencer, and that is a valid expression of leadership with which I am comfortable, and for which I believe God has gifted me. Therefore, I am happiest in the role of serving churches and organisations by developing their personnel, rather than in leading them from the front.

As I look back, I can see that during what became an action-packed period I was operating in several different spheres of ministry at the same time, each distinct and yet overlapping and interconnected. Each sphere was an expansion of what I was already doing. Life was full and very satisfying, if exhausting at times.

Retreats

My retreat work centred around the strong connections I had made already at Ashburnham Place and Penhurst Retreat Centre (both in Sussex), but also included newer venues for me like Nicholaston House in Wales, Scargill House in Yorkshire, and El Palmeral in Spain. I also made new links in Northern Ireland, often working with church leaders, and finding there a deep hunger for intimacy with God. The focus of my retreats (usually four or five days long) has always been on developing intimacy with God, built around the exposition of a theme from the Bible, contemplative worship, times for personal reflection, rest, and, if desired, an opportunity for spiritual accompaniment. There are other ways to lead retreats, but this approach suited my gifting and attracted others for whom a Bible-focused, Christ-centred approach was important. I emphasised the place of stillness, silence, and solitude as the way to draw near to God, and Bible meditation, personal reflection, and contemplation as the means of going deeper in our relationship with him.

If ever I thought leading retreats was a soft option, I soon realised it was not, and in fact it brought me into the realm of spiritual warfare. Satan resists the attempts of God's people to become intimate with him, since he knows that 'the people that do know their God shall be strong' (Daniel 11:32, KJV), and Satan seeks to disrupt that process. It was surprising how often people got sick before they were due to come on retreat, how many things went wrong in the build-up, and how under attack I often found myself beforehand. All this seemed more than coincidence and felt more like a direct attempt by the Devil to hinder the work of God. Yet time and again I saw the value of making space to be with God as lives were healed and transformed simply by leisurely spending time in his presence and allowing the Spirit to do his work. A few days away from normal routine in a conducive environment brought refreshment for body and soul, a clarity in hearing God's voice, a new awareness of the love of God, and a greater openness to change. Regular time for retreat is highly recommended!

Writing

Most of my writing flowed out of the teaching I gave on retreat. I found that God would give me a theme for the year ahead which I would explore and study for myself, then teach to others. Having used the material for a couple of years, modified and improved it, I could then turn it into book form. *A Fruitful Life* (2006) came out of retreats based on John 15, *Working From a Place of Rest* (2010) from looking closely at John 4, *Servant Ministry* (2013) from a study of Isaiah 42, and *Deep Calls to Deep* (2015) from my work on the Psalms of lament. If I have a gift in writing it is to make complicated truth accessible to ordinary people, and to express my thoughts clearly with relevance to everyday life.

In many ways my writing mirrors my own spiritual journey, especially my hunger to become more like Jesus and be more effective in serving him. My focus is almost entirely on the inner life, which is unusual these days when most Christian books are pragmatic in outlook – how to build a bigger church, how to be a better leader, how to make more disciples, and so on. Previous generations seemed to value a deeper spirituality, reflective in approach and instructive in knowing God more intimately. I feel my writing has been prophetic as I sense God calling his church to develop inwardness as the basis and foundation of a life given to service and activity.

Two books came about in a different way, however. For a while I worked closely with Dr Debbie Hawker, a clinical psychologist and specialist in debriefing and trauma counselling. We led several retreats together at Penhurst and collaborated on a writing project to produce *Resilience in Life and Faith* (2019). Debbie provided practical teaching on how to develop resilience, and I contributed chapters looking at the associated biblical teaching and examples from scripture of men and women who showed great perseverance in their faith. The book was very well received, coming out as it did just before the Covid pandemic, and has been translated into several languages already.

The other book was also written in collaboration, this time with a team of five other writers. Even before the pandemic I was feeling within myself a longing to know Jesus more deeply by spending time in the gospel story. The idea came of a devotional with a focus on spiritual formation that would look at the life of Jesus chronologically, bringing the four accounts of his life together into a coherent whole. I was inspired by the prayer of Richard of Chichester (1197–1253) that we might see Jesus more clearly, love him more dearly, and follow him more nearly. My intention was to write the devotionals myself but having spent such a long time on the chronology of the story, and then breaking it down into 365 daily portions, I decided I needed help with the writing!

Knowing You, Jesus (2023) is an invitation to spend a year in the company of Jesus and thus to be changed and transformed. Again, there is a prophetic edge to the book. I feel the danger of the contemporary church, with all its busyness and activity, is to lose sight of Jesus, relegating him to the periphery of church life. *Knowing You, Jesus* is therefore a call to come back to the central purpose of our faith – to be with Jesus, and then to be sent out from him.

I love the whole process of writing, and beavering away in my garden office feeds my introversion as well as my love of study. It is the place where I most easily encounter God. I marvel at how words come together and ideas take shape to create something that will hopefully continue to speak to people long after I am gone. When I write I feel I am in God's presence. Yes, it is hard work, and it takes a long time to produce a manuscript, but for me it is life-giving, a form of communion with God. Mostly writers know little of the impact their words have on others, but occasionally we hear, and what a joy that is!

None of this would have been possible without one of those 'chance' meetings which have been characteristic of how God has led me. I happened to meet Karen Laister of the Bible Reading Fellowship (now known as BRF Ministries) at a Booksellers' Convention in Doncaster way back in 2001. I was there to promote my first ever book, *The Call to Intimacy*, and she asked for a copy. Soon afterwards I received a letter from Naomi Starkey, at that time the commissioning editor, inviting me to write for them, and I have been doing so ever since – both books and daily Bible reading notes. I am so grateful to have a publisher who believes in me as a writer, and who has been willing to publish so many of my books. I could never have forged such a relationship myself. Only God could do that!

Mentoring

Another thread is woven through my entire adult life – that of mentoring others. My simple definition of mentoring is this: promoting the work of God in the life of another. From my early years in Borneo, part of my remit was to develop younger, local leaders in line with Paul's ministry philosophy: 'The things you have heard me say in the presence of many witnesses entrust to reliable people who will also be qualified to teach others' (2 Timothy 2:2). This passing on of the baton is a crucial part of Christian leadership. In all that we do, whether in mission or local church leadership, we should have one eye on the development and growth of those around us, helping them to identify their gifts and releasing them into the ministry God has for them.

I was instinctively mentoring other people, but my understanding of the process was increased by learning from Rick Lewis, an Australian pastor who came over to the UK to lead seminars on mentoring and came to Bawtry Hall during my time there. He introduced me to the work of John Mallison, an Australian minister whose book *Mentoring to Develop Disciples and Leaders* (Scripture Union, 1999) became something of a textbook for us.

From that point on I was more intentional about mentoring and gave time both formally and informally to many of those I met in the course of my work who needed encouragement, guidance, or simply a listening ear. Having read widely about the topic, and gained experience over several years, I wrote *Mentoring for Spiritual Growth* (2008). It reflected the overlap in my own thinking and practice between discipleship and spiritual direction, and was slanted towards providing an understanding of the spiritual journey for those who were mentoring others.

Realising the importance of mentoring in Christian discipleship and knowing the hunger that many of those offering mentoring had to be further equipped for the task, I invited a small group to come together for a few days of mutual encouragement and learning. We called it

The Mentoring Forum, and we met annually at a conference centre in Derbyshire from 2008 until the Covid pandemic brought things to a natural end. We had many inspiring times together, broadening our understanding of the Christian life, and experiencing a variety of spiritual practices from different Christian traditions.

Singapore

All this time I was also heavily involved with the churches in Singapore. At first this was rather piecemeal and not really building anything that would last. As I thought about this, and talked with others, the idea came to develop a mentoring programme especially for Singapore, that would take a small group of believers and work with them over a two-year period to encourage their growth in God and their experience of contemplative spirituality. I developed a curriculum and committed myself to visit Singapore three times a year.

So in August 2007 we launched the Mentoring Programme. This would not have been possible without the help of Grace Lim who offered to be the administrator for the programme. Christopher and Michelle Tan gave us the use of their beautiful home as a place to meet. They had recently renovated their house to be a place of retreat for those in ministry, and as well as graciously welcoming us to The Nest (as they called it), kindly offered me accommodation whenever I was in Singapore. What a provision, and what an encouragement from God!

About 25 people signed up for the first course and about the same number for the second, a mixture of church leaders and active lay people. The programme consisted of reading assignments, teaching days, tutorials, the opportunity to attend Quiet Days, and have personal time, either with myself or one of the team of helpers I had assembled. It was amazing to see how people flourished in this setting and became secure in their identity as God's deeply loved children.

After two cohorts had been through the course, we changed tack and focused on biannual retreats, held in the green and pleasant surroundings of a golfing hotel just over the border in Malaysia. These were wonderful times of teaching and instruction, with rich fellowship as we shared our lives together, as well as the journey of following Jesus. This was a faith venture, with no set fees, but the generosity of Singaporean believers is well known, and I found my travel costs were more than covered by their generous gifts. Along the way, many deep friendships were formed among the participants.

As well as the mentoring programme, I was able to work with churches like St John's and St Margaret's (Anglican) and Bartley Christian Church (independent), which became my adopted spiritual home in Singapore. It was a special joy to work closely with OMF Singapore and to find healing from my previous difficulties with the mission. I will always be grateful to God for this period of my life, so rich in blessing and being able to do that for which I was most fitted.

Caring for missionaries

There was one further significant strand to ministry in this phase – the opportunity to serve as pastoral care person for MAF Europe, supporting their teams in their Africa programmes. This was a natural extension of my involvement in the orientation courses for their new workers and gave me the opportunity to see how they were doing on the field. My brief was simple – to spend time with the international staff in each programme, to encourage their well-being, and then provide spiritual input for them as a group to strengthen them in their service for God.

This meant a lot of travel and exposure to a new part of the world for me. From 2008 to 2013, I paid over 20 visits to different teams in Kenya, Uganda, Tanzania, Chad, Sudan, and Madagascar. It was good for me to face culture shock again, and to be in a vulnerable position myself as one also needing help and support. I found Africa so different from

Southeast Asia, which I knew so well. I remember vividly on my first visit being visually impacted by the large numbers of people walking alongside the main roads, the red dust from the ground swirling around, and the chaotic driving and traffic noise. There always seemed to be an edge of uncertainty in the African cities I visited, and as a westerner I felt a little unsafe. The welcome, however, from the MAF staff (local and international) was always warm and reassuring and this helped in my adjustment. Gradually I fell into the rhythm of Africa, although I was never fully relaxed there.

I have always had a heart for 'member care', that is the support of those in cross-cultural mission, so again I was in my element. It was in some ways a boyhood adventure come true, as I got to fly many times into the rural areas alongside the MAF pilots. Experiencing first-hand the pressures of life on a compound was instructive, and the stress of living with constant uncertainty (unreliable electricity supply, political upheaval, and food shortages, for example) informed my understanding of the needs. I loved meeting the African staff, so vibrant in their faith and happy in their disposition, but I saw for myself how cultural differences made for misunderstandings in the working environment. And always there was the tension of being a relatively 'rich' person in a world where most others were poor. Add to this, concerns for children's schooling and elderly relatives back home, plus the dangers inherent in flying in Africa, and you get a feel of the daily challenges faced by mission personnel.

My conviction is that if we have a strong spiritual foundation, we can cope better with the challenges that life throws at us, so we gradually began to introduce Quiet Days, and in some programmes, time away for retreat. These not only bolstered the bonds between staff but also helped them build a stable connection with God that would keep them steady in the continual changes they had to navigate. In all of this, I constantly felt out of my depth and in need of God's help, a good place to be but not always a comfortable one. Yet what a privilege to see so much of the world and to broaden my own horizons.

If you are feeling exhausted after reading all that, so am I! Looking back, I am not sure how I managed to carry such a load. It was only possible because of the grace of God at work within me, but such a pace could not be sustained indefinitely. It was for a season, and that season began to come to an end as I reached retirement age (2015) and began to let go of some of my responsibilities. Other factors would soon enter my life that would bring me to a complete standstill and lead to a major change of direction.

Reflection 10:

WORKING FROM A PLACE OF REST

As you have been reading through my story you will notice that working from a place of rest is a recurring theme, indicating both my journey into understanding the importance of this, and also the difficulty of putting it into practice!

One day, as I followed my daily reading programme, I came to a familiar passage in John 4 which recounts the meeting of Jesus with the Samaritan woman. I remember it vividly. I was speaking at a mission centre in the south of England, sitting on my bed in the sparsely furnished room, as I waited to go for the first session. This story is often used to teach the principles of personal evangelism, and to be honest, I approached the passage with an air of tedium. Yet as I started to read my eyes were opened to a whole new way of understanding the passage. Insight seemed to come to me in waves, and one thought led to another as I felt the Holy Spirit teaching me and showing me the way that Jesus did ministry.

The words of verse 6 seemed to be highlighted for me and became the focus of my attention: 'Jacob's well was there, and Jesus, tired as he was from the journey, sat down by the well. It was about noon.'

The first thought to hit me was that *Jesus was doing nothing*. It was midday and he was sitting by the well, taking a rest. They had started their journey early in the morning and now in the heat of the mid-day sun it was time to find a shady spot to rest and be refreshed, a natural enough response. What struck me, however, was the fact that Jesus was doing nothing. That seemed incongruous for the one who had come to save the world and had only a few short years in which to accomplish his task. Surely, he should be using his time more profitably.

Then, almost immediately, came a second associated thought: *everything that happens in this story happened because Jesus was doing nothing.* If he hadn't been taking a breather, he would not have met the Samaritan woman. If he hadn't been in an unhurried frame of mind, he would not have had time to talk with her, and if they hadn't had the conversation then the woman would not have been awakened in her faith and revival would not have come to that sleepy Samaritan village. All this happens because Jesus was doing nothing, having a rest, taking a break. I felt there was something very significant here for me as I watched how Jesus went about his ministry.

Even as I pondered this, a third insight popped into my mind: if this was how Jesus operated, *we too can learn to work from a place of rest.* By taking a break Jesus was endorsing the validity and importance of rest and showing us that the Father is at work even when we are not. The kingdom does not come by the power of human effort alone, but by the initiative of God. We are invited to join in what he is already doing. This takes all the strain and effort out of it because the work is God's, not ours. At that point in my ministry this was revolutionary thinking. I scribbled down some notes and went off to the meeting.

Over the next few days, I continued to meditate on this passage and on verse 6 in particular. I saw two other key things. Firstly, that *Jesus became tired as he travelled*, a clear indication of the reality of his humanity. Even the Son of God expended energy as he lived and worked, had limits to what he could do, and required space to re-energise. His example gives us permission to acknowledge our own tiredness and need to pause so that we can be restored. He gives us permission to rest. It is legitimate to acknowledge our limitations and not feel that we must keep going all the time.

Then I was struck by the word *journey*. Jesus was on a journey from Jerusalem in the south to Galilee in the north. He was also, as the gospel of John points out, on a much greater journey which brought him from heaven to earth and would eventually lead him back from earth to heaven (John 16:28). I love the word journey as a metaphor for the Christian life. It so aptly describes a lifetime of following, and the different stages we pass through. We can say that it is legitimate to feel tired on the journey – the journey through life, the journey of discipleship, and the journey of transformation.

These five points became integral to my thinking, and I sought to apply them to my own life and then share them with others under the heading 'Working from a place of rest'. Eventually this became the title of a book published by BRF Ministries in 2010 and one which has impacted many people's lives, especially those in ministry. I am sure not all the thoughts were my own; probably they are a distillation of the things I had been reading about already but was feeling and engaging with for myself.

In the light of what I had discovered, I began to be more deliberate in looking after myself, making sure I got sufficient rest and did not overcommit myself. I began to realise that we are to establish rest in God as the foundation of our life, and work from that place rather than into it – in other words, to see rest as the basis for effort, not the reward for when the work is done. I daily asked God to teach me that this was his work and to help me not to strive to make things happen but to trust that he would be at work through me.

Not that this was easy, and I found I went in and out of rest and still do. It was so natural to become overextended, taking on more than I had the capacity to manage. I often fell back into my old patterns of hard work, conscientiousness, and self-effort. Yet there was a difference, and I have found since that when I remember to pace myself and manage my workload there is an ease in ministry that was not there before. Perhaps this will always be a struggle, and I am comfortable with that. I don't always get it right, and that's okay. I am still learning.

Point of connection

It has been said that our best contribution in ministry comes in the second half of life. For this reason, our 50s and 60s can be the most fulfilling years of all when we make our greatest contribution. Although energy is decreasing, we now have wisdom on our side, and we know how to work according to our strongest gifts while depending on God more than ever.

You may not have reached this stage yet, but some of the insights given here will still be relevant to you. It may be helpful to talk to more experienced believers who are clearly enjoying ministry and bearing much fruit at this stage of life. What have they discovered that helps them to sustain their ministry effectiveness?

- What do you consider to be the difference between a 'productive' life and a 'fruitful' life?

- In the narrative section I identify five strands in my ministry during these years. What would you say are the main thrusts in what you are called to do? Why does it help to identify these clearly?

- Self-care is not a luxury but a necessity; it is not being selfish but expressing wisdom. It is how we sustain ourselves for the long haul of ministry. How do you currently practise self-care? Are you satisfied that you are looking after your own body, soul, and spirit adequately?

- Consider the five insights that came to me from John 4. Relate each one to your own situation and approach to ministry. What do you learn from this?

If you wish, on your timeline include some of the key verses of scripture that have been foundational for you, and those that have been guiding lights when you needed direction.

11

CONTRACTING

Even though I walk through the darkest valley, I will fear no evil, for you are with me; your rod and your staff, they comfort me.

PSALM 23:4

I've come to realise that any experience of loss or bereavement can run a canon ball through the most robust faith. Indeed, through our very being.

Mary Hippsley[39]

In his book, *The Space Between*, Mark Bradford writes about the disruptive seasons of life, triggered, for example, by a serious illness, the end of a close relationship, the death of a loved one, the loss of a job or income, or the failure of a longing to be realised. He uses five metaphors to describe such periods: *the time of waiting* (when life is put on hold); *the place of exile* (when life feels alien); *the wilderness* (when life is stripped back); *the storm* (when life is shaken); and *the pit* (when life sinks to the bottom).[40]

Dr J. Robert Clinton, in his studies of leadership formation, speaks in a similar vein about such life transitions as 'boundary time' when significant disorientation, brokenness, and refinement come into our story, and we find ourselves in a crucible of transformation. These periods of crisis hold the possibility of profoundly altering the shape and direction of a person's life and are usually associated with a heightened time of learning.[41] God often uses such times to move us from one phase of life to another.

The next few years of my life (2018–21) could well be described as a disruptive season or as boundary time, but the metaphor I would use would be that of *the cave* – entering a dark place of confinement and restriction and experiencing a period of isolation from the usual pattern of life and ministry. What caused all this? Evelyn's terminal illness, the coming of the worldwide Covid pandemic, and my own brush with death.

The darkness descends

As I passed my retirement age (65), I had no thoughts of stopping work entirely, only of slowing down and doing less international travel. This decision was fuelled partly by the awareness that I was getting older, but also by the fact that Evelyn had a recurrence of breast cancer. She had first been diagnosed in 2010, but after surgery, chemotherapy, and radiation treatment, had enjoyed some happy years of remission. Then, in 2016 the cancer suddenly reappeared, and she faced over the next four years, another lengthy period of gruelling chemotherapy. At first, I tried to combine a lighter workload with supporting her, but eventually felt I needed to give as much time to be with her as possible and so in 2018 I stopped most of what I was doing, especially anything that took me away from home.

Evelyn was never an upfront person but expressed her faith and her love through her actions. She had a particular gift in working with elderly, mentally ill patients, and had worked as a senior staff nurse in several local nursing homes. Perhaps her greatest achievement was in establishing locally a Christian care home (called Warde Aldham) for the organisation Trinity Care, where she was the first matron. Her calm manner meant that those around her were also calm, and this greatly enhanced her work. It also meant that she faced her own illness with courage and a quiet confidence, trusting God for the difficult journey she was on. Much of our time was spent on hospital appointments and trips to the A&E when things became too bad. In a strange way, these times were special and drew us closer together.

Into the cave

At the start of 2020 we were told that the cancer had moved into her spine and her condition was terminal. She was given only 'months' to live, a very sobering truth to receive. We were coming up to my 70th birthday in March and decided to have a small celebration with our close family and friends, which we did despite the awareness that Covid was closing in on us all. Evelyn was well enough to attend and see many of these special people for the last time. The very next day the first lockdown began in the UK, and we were on our own.

At first my daughter Debbie and I tried to care for Evelyn at home, but as her condition worsened, we were advised she needed nursing care, and there was a place in the local hospice. We decided that I would go with her, otherwise, because of Covid restrictions, I would not be able to see her. After a week of expert care her condition improved and we were told she would have to be transferred either back home, or to a local care home where nursing care was available. For various reasons we decided to go together into a local care home, even though we knew Covid was now rampant in such facilities. We could not have managed at home by ourselves. It was a big decision, but we felt it was the right one. So reluctantly, we moved into Cherry Trees, a care home on the edge of Barnsley – Evelyn into the nursing wing, and me to the residential unit.

I have told the detailed story of our time there in my book *Finding Refuge* (self-published, 2020) so here will condense my account. We had eight weeks together, which gave us opportunity to talk about many things and to say all that we needed to say. It was a strange environment for me, but we gradually adapted to the noise, heat, and strange happenings. Not being able to have visitors made the days seem long, and being confined to the building meant that the beautiful spring weather enjoyed by others passed us by. Inevitably, Covid came into the home, and we both succumbed to the virus. Evelyn quickly recovered, but I got worse. I was confined to my tiny, airless room, and could see Evelyn for only an hour a day. As my condition deteriorated, I felt I needed to be at home, and after discussing it with Evelyn, we agreed I should do that.

I had no idea how ill I was. Debbie came to help me get home, but after a couple of days she realised I was seriously ill and called for an ambulance. I was rushed into the local hospital and soon found myself in the intensive care unit, fighting for my life. I was so conscious of the prayers of many people for both me and Evelyn, but the medics were clear that for me it could go either way. I was placed in an oxygen hood for intensive oxygen therapy (CPAP) and told if this did not work it would mean a ventilator. I remember it was Pentecost Sunday, and I prayed that the breath of God would enter my lungs and bring healing. Eventually, the crisis period passed, and I turned the corner to recovery. After nearly two weeks I was back home again and regaining my strength.

Sadly, I was not allowed to return to the care home, which was difficult for me as I felt I had failed to be with Evelyn at her neediest hour. As I troubled over this, I sensed God say, 'She was mine long before she was yours, and I won't let her down now.' Although Evelyn had a few more weeks, she became quite confused and eventually passed away on 13 July 2020. Debbie and I, with Evelyn's brother Ian, were with her over her last weekend. Her final words were, 'Thank you Jesus, you led me all the way.'

Cold days, heavy heart

Grieving during lockdown was hard, with none of the usual support available. Because Evelyn had chosen to be buried, people could attend the graveside funeral, but socially distanced, and no hugging.

Close family came back to the house, but there was no opportunity to meet with others. We held a thanksgiving over Zoom so we could see friends from around the world. Then it was back to the rigours of isolation and lockdown.

I journalled a lot during the next year, part of my way of coping with the loss. I was grateful to have the wise counsel of Dr Bill Webster, a friend from my days at London Bible College, who lives in Canada and is internationally respected as a grief counsellor. We chatted over the internet fortnightly for many months, where Bill patiently helped me to understand the grief journey and to make sense of life without Evelyn. I also talked regularly with Dr Debbie Hawker (see chapter 10), and it was at those times that my tears flowed most freely. I joined an online grief course and read widely for myself about grief and loss. I felt that understanding the process would help me cope, and it did.

One sentence from Bill seemed to sum up perfectly my experience of grief. He writes, 'There is possibly no more difficult experience than to lose someone you have loved and cared about. There is no greater loss than to be separated from someone who loved you and cared about you.'[42] These words pierced my heart. I felt I could continue to love Evelyn, albeit in a different way than before, but who was there to love me now in return? It felt like having a hole in my heart, and I could see no way in which it could be healed. As the weeks passed, the dark and cold of winter seemed to mirror the darkness and coldness I felt within.

Joy in the morning

With the help of some loyal friends, I began to adjust to the practicalities of life on my own, but it was far from easy. Some came and taught me how to cook for myself, others met me for walks in the countryside, even on gloomy November days. My grief journey had its ups and downs, and I made mistakes. Eventually spring came, and then a lifting of Covid restrictions. Slowly, hope began to return, and I began to think of what I would do with my life. A new day was dawning.

I had the sense of God saying to me that I had one more adventure to live, which I understood to mean another season of life in which to serve him and bear fruit. I am sure that having a sense of purpose was vital to my recovery. I did not want to get stuck in my grief, so with God's help I determined to take hold again of his purpose for my life. This does not imply that I stopped loving or grieving, only that after bereavement there is still a life to be lived. I had recovered well from Covid, and as the anniversary of Evelyn's death approached, felt I was physically back to normal. Even the diabetes that came on because of the treatment I received (steroids) had cleared up, all part of the miracle that was my recovery.

The whole experience of losing Evelyn and nearly losing my own life had given me a new awareness that life is fragile and must be lived to the full, that we must seize the moment and not take anything for granted. Every day seemed precious, a gift which is not to be wasted. Time itself felt different. Not an endless stream coming towards me, but a resource that was fast running out. Unless you have been there, this heightened sense of the gift of life and the need to make the most of the time may be hard to understand, but it was very much how I felt.

A more detailed account of my grief journey, some key things I learned from the experience of grief counselling, and how the scriptures informed my journey is given in my book *Grief Notes: Walking through loss* (2022). Grief is unique to each person, but there are some similarities, and we can learn from each other. Now, some five years further on, I can see what a watershed moment I had been through, one that would change my life in ways I could never have imagined. It had indeed been a time of intense learning, and a passage into a new adventure with God. My life had contracted but was about to expand again.

Reflection 11:

THE CHANGING SCENES OF LIFE

Our lives are in a state of constant flux, and no matter how much we may value stability, change is inevitable. Our normal patterns of living get disrupted, and we must learn to adjust to new circumstances and adapt accordingly. Fortunately, as human beings we are created to be adaptive, and as we go through life, we learn strategies to cope with change, although life's disruptions can still be stressful and destabilising.

The worldwide Covid pandemic brought unprecedented change (remember that phrase?) into all our lives, and a great deal of hardship and suffering. It required us at short notice to adjust to new ways of living, working, and communicating which at first seemed impossible. However, gradually a new normal was established and life continued despite lockdowns and the restrictions of social distancing. We got used to wearing face masks, washing our hands fastidiously, and, of course, using Zoom. Now we can look back and see many ways in which our lives have been permanently shaped by that experience. We adapted, and a new way was established.

Pandemics aside, we still routinely face many changes, less dramatic but still challenging. What sort of things in the ordinary course of life might lead us into a period of change?

The *stages of life* call for change. We move through childhood and the teenage years into adulthood, then midlife before entering our later years and eventually old age. Each stage has its own unique challenges, needs, and opportunities that require us to adapt our behaviour if we are to live well.

Life events create change – starting school, leaving home, getting married (or remaining single), becoming parents then grandparents, caring for elderly relatives, and maybe grandchildren. Each change invites significant adjustment.

Crises may unexpectedly come our way – bereavements, relationship breakdowns, redundancies, poor health, accidents, and so on, all rock the boat and throw us into confusion, and necessitate courage and flexibility.

Some changes we choose, but even good changes can be stressful – moving house, changing jobs, relocating, retraining, and so on, may all be welcome but demand a suppleness of approach.

Constant change, it seems, is here to stay. Fortunately, while change is inevitable and unavoidable, there is a pattern to change, and moving from one phase of life to another (what we call transition) is a predictable process which we can identify and understand. This awareness can then help us to navigate periods of change more effectively.

A cursory reading of my own storyline will show many times of change and transition, some welcomed, others not. Missionary life is full of transitions, but what I did not realise was that bereavement itself is a transition experience. Only when I was well into the grieving process did I became aware that perhaps I could use the skills I had learned through my missionary experience in rebuilding my life and adjusting to the new norm of life without Evelyn. I was unaware then that the rebuilding process would soon require me to navigate another major transition, albeit a very happy one, involving a complete reordering of my life and a major relocation from one part of the country to another. More of that later!

Most of us will be able to identify seasons of change in our lives, many of them enjoyable, others disturbing and disorientating. Change may be defined as the disruption caused by alterations to the equilibrium of life. The normal flow of life as we know it is interrupted, and we are called upon to adjust and adapt, and discover a new normal. Transition describes the process of navigating change and passing smoothly from one phase or period of life to another until equilibrium is established again.

No transition is without a sense of upheaval and emotional turmoil. Uncertainty and ambiguity are uncomfortable feelings, and the space between the old normal and the new can be chaotic and frightening. It is normal to feel stressed at such times, even overwhelmed, as we long for stability and rootedness. All change involves loss of some kind, for we must let go of the old before we can take hold of the new. Loss is the separation from people, places, and things that have meaning for us that occurs as we go through change. Grief describes the cluster of emotions we feel during such times of loss, in particular sadness, regret, anguish, and despair.

A normal transition process

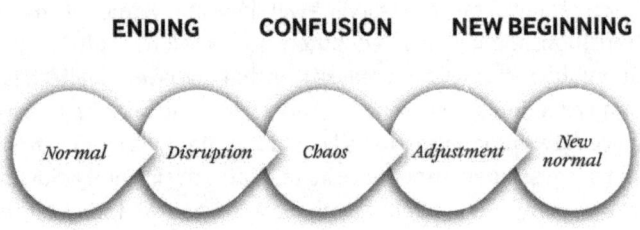

A major transition can take up to two years

In this diagram we can see the five stages that we typically pass through in a time of transition. Life is never as smooth as a diagram, and we often move backwards and forwards, and not always in the exact order as shown, but generally this is the pattern. A disruptive event (good or bad) brings an ending to a phase of life, requiring us to let go of our old way of living. There follows a period of uncertainty when we are betwixt and between, having left but not yet arrived. Gradually we adjust to a different pattern of life and eventually a new way of being and doing is established and we feel at ease again in the new situation which slowly feels like normal.

It can take two years or more for major transitions to work themselves through, and the impact of transition upon us is largely due to how we feel about the change. If the change is something we have chosen, that we feel good about, and have some control over then it will be less impactful than a change we have not chosen, do not welcome, and have little power over.

How can we best prepare ourselves for transition?

Clearly, the more we can prepare ourselves in advance for change, the easier it will be. Understanding the process helps enormously and thinking ahead will help us in anticipating how we might feel at certain moments, so we are not taken by surprise when we suddenly feel afraid, or bereft, or anxious. Such feelings are normal, and they will eventually pass. I have found balancing the 'gains' with the 'losses' in any transition keeps me from being too negative. Choosing to be grateful for what is, rather than focusing on what is not, creates a positive mindset, as does rejoicing in what we still have rather than lamenting what we hvae lost. Although the way ahead may not be too clear, allowing ourselves to feel excited about what is to come will cause thankfulness to grow within us, rather than our being stuck in grumbling or complaining.

Transition takes time, and it is important that we are patient throughout the process. When life is disrupted, it can feel as if all the pieces that make up the jigsaw of our life have been broken up and thrown into the air. We must wait for them to come down again and then reassemble the picture piece by piece. This is especially so when there is a geographical relocation, as happens so often for missionaries and those whose work or ministry causes them to move around. From finding where to live, schools for the children, a new church, where best to shop, setting up health care, and making new friends, there are many pieces of the jigsaw that may need to be reassembled during a big move.

During such upheaval it is helpful if we can exercise our trust in God, who is the one constant when life is in flux. Although God is a dynamic God, who often initiates change and is often doing a 'new thing' (Isaiah 42:9, 43:18–19, Revelation 21:5), he is also a stable God whose character does not change and who is always faithful to his word. He is our rock, and he remains steady in his love for us, holding us in the grip of his grace when everything around us is shaking (Malachi 3:6, Psalm 18:1–2). He will lead and guide us, provide for us, and bring us safely to the place where he wants us to be. We can turn to him at any time and tell him how we feel, and receive his strength for each and every day.

It may help to talk to someone who understands the transition process and who has perhaps walked a similar path before us. This is a good time to find a listening ear – a pastoral carer, a mentor, a counsellor, or a spiritual director. Such people can provide a safe place for us to share our concerns and offer good advice when we feel we are not coping so well.

It is often only when we are through a transition and can look back on the period of change that we can, with hindsight, see the hand of God has been at work. God has the amazing ability to cause everything (even that which is not good) to work together for good (Romans 8:28) and he weaves all things into his perfect plan for our life. This is true even when we find ourselves kicking and screaming against what is happening. God is patient and forbearing with us, and gently accomplishes his will for us.

In his book *The Land Between*, pastor and author Jeff Manion writes about how we can find God in difficult transitions, which he describes as 'prime real estate for transformation'. He recognises that if our responses are unguarded, we may become bitter and cynical, but if we turn to God for help, such a time 'is fertile ground for our spiritual transformation and for God's grace to be revealed in magnificent ways'.[43] Clearly, we have a choice to make. We can be resistant or responsive to what God is doing within us. Hopefully we find the grace to allow God to shape and form us during our seasons of transition – deepening our trust, creating the space that dependency gives for him to work, and conforming us to the likeness of his Son.

Point of connection

Ageing brings its own challenges, and the later years of our discipleship journey will reflect this. We may have health issues (or care for someone who has); experience the loss of those closest to us; struggle with our mental agility and with a body that is slowing down. We may not always be able to operate as we did before, and this can come as a shock to us. Some will sail through their 70s with little apparent change, but for many this will be a bumpy road when our faith will be tested in new ways and our human limitations revealed.

This may not be your life stage yet, but it will be that of many people around you. It is worth trying to understand what the journey is like for them so you can support and encourage them, while at the same time grow in your understanding for when you travel through this difficult terrain yourself.

- What has been for you a disruptive season? Does it fit into one of Bradford's five categories, or does it need a metaphor of its own?

- What can you learn from my experience of 'the cave'? How can these insights help to build your own resilience?

- As you look back on a 'boundary time', what exactly happened? Was it for you a time of heightened learning? If so, in what ways?

- What has been your experience of grief and loss so far? How have you experienced God's presence in your grief journey? What have you learned about the experience of grieving? Has grieving changed your perspective on life?

- 'Life events create change.' How has life called for you to adapt and adjust? What have you found helpful in times of change and transition?

- Where do you see God at work in this stage of your life?

If you would like, on your timeline identify times of transition, and take note of any feelings that arise as you ponder the changes you have been through, whether welcomed or resisted.

12
EMERGING

He brought me out into a spacious place; he rescued me because he delighted in me.

PSALM 18:19

God loves us with a passionate love. It is too great for us to comprehend; we do not have words to describe it fully. It is too vast to grasp completely. *But we can know it. We can feel it.*

James Bryan Smith[44]

Throughout the dark months of bereavement and loss, I had struggled to trust God for my future. I tried in vain to trust but still felt anxious and a little afraid. Then, during a conversation with a friend about this specific difficulty, I had a moment of insight – trusting God is not about our ability to trust, but the fact that he is worthy of our trust. He is a trustworthy God. Whether we feel we can trust or not, he will remain faithful to us and will bring us through.

Hope returns

I remembered that my great hero, the missionary Hudson Taylor, had translated Mark 11:22 as 'Hold the faithfulness of God' (the emphasis on God), rather than 'Have faith in God' (the emphasis on me). This is a valid translation and recalling it helped me to take my eyes off myself and place them where they belonged, fully upon Jesus. Another scripture came to my help as well: 'If we are faithless, he remains faithful, for he cannot disown himself' (2 Timothy 2:13). Our confidence is not in ourselves, but in the character of God, and even if we let God down, he will never fail us. As this truth sank into my heavy heart, light began to shine into my soul again and I felt I could trust him for my future.

On another occasion, two people on the same day shared with me the verse above from Psalm 18:19, and it resonated strongly within me. I knew that God delighted in me. I was keenly aware that he had rescued me from Covid. Now, I began to believe that he would, in due course, bring me into a spacious place, a place of freedom of movement where there is room to grow. The promised land was often described as 'a spacious place' and I took it to mean a good place, a place that God had in mind for me, where I would flourish again.

The way opens up

Slowly, as things opened up again after the pandemic, I began to step back into ministry, albeit gingerly. As I pondered the way ahead, I sensed the next phase of life would be less busy but still significant, with four strands to my life. Writing would now be my priority, with retreat work taking second place, and then time for friendship, and finally time to travel. I was not sure how this would work out, but it helped to have a plan in mind even if I held it lightly.

I took a personal retreat at Penhurst where these thoughts began to crystallise, and it was there that someone described me as 'an elder statesman', which I took as a compliment and encouragement for my role going forward, into my 70s. This is the phase I am now in. Dr J. Robert Clinton has very little to say about the later years of life but does describe it as the 'Afterglow' or 'Celebration' period where 'the fruit of a lifetime of ministry and growth culminates in an era of recognition and indirect influence at broad levels'.[45]

Janet Hagberg and Robert Guelich have more to say, describing ministry through the later years as 'The Life of Love' when 'we reflect God to others in the world more clearly and consistently than we ever thought possible.'[46] It is a period when we are more at peace with ourselves and, freed from personal ambition, able to focus more on the development of others. We continue to be Spirit-filled in an unassuming way, and are content to live a simple life, which is Christ-centred and happily obedient to God. Wisdom gained from life's struggles gives us compassionate insight to help younger leaders. At least that is the theory. It is certainly my aspiration, though others are better placed to say how well it describes me!

A time to flourish

Our later years need not be barren years. Health issues could be a major factor limiting our contribution, but the psalmist is in no doubt that we can both flourish and bear fruit: 'The righteous will flourish like a palm tree, they will grow like a cedar of Lebanon; planted in the house of the Lord, they will flourish in the courts of our God. They will still bear fruit in old age, they will stay fresh and green, proclaiming, "The Lord is upright; he is my Rock, and there is no wickedness in him"'(Psalm 92:12–15). We may not do as much as before, but what we do can still be effective. We may not lead from the front, but we can be a great support to those who do. We can continue to have influence.

A major event in this period for me has been the God-given opportunity to be married again. Evelyn had said to me that I should remarry, knowing how much I need companionship and support, and her encouragement has released me and helped me to take another step in the adventure with God. I prayed so much that God would guide me in this matter. Knowing I would first need to grieve well to be ready for a new relationship, I took time to explore this area of my life before God, using David Benner's book *Surrender to Love* (IVP, 2003) to heal my heart and find my security once again in my identity as God's deeply loved child.

Second spring

My Chinese friends describe remarriage as a second spring, a time when love blossoms again and there is a fresh start in life. Not everyone who loses a spouse wants to remarry, and for good reasons, but some do, and I was one. To find again a person whom you love, and who loves you in return, is no easy matter. If it happens, then it is indeed a special blessing. I was favoured in this way when Jilly came into my life.

I had known Jilly for some years, but we were not in regular contact until the summer of 2021. She worked for many years as a nurse and midwife, then retrained as a counsellor and has developed an expertise in helping those with traumatic backgrounds. After the break-up of her first marriage, she brought up her two sons by herself, and since they had now graduated and married, she was also in a new phase of life. We share many things in common, but a love for retreat and the contemplative tradition was important to both of us. The big obstacle was that we lived at opposite ends of the country, Jilly on the south coast in Bournemouth, and me over 200 miles away in Yorkshire. Thank God for Zoom!

There were many journeys north to south (and south to north) as we got to know each other. I also lived with a family from Jilly's church for two months so we could spend more time together and develop our relationship in the normalities of daily life. Gradually, after many confirmations, we became sure that this relationship was a gift from God to us both, and we were married in June 2022. Our families were all happy for us, which helped our decision-making enormously. Friends who knew us well could also see that we were well suited and that our gifts were complementary. It may have happened a little quickly for some but being of more mature years, and aware of the fragility of life, we wanted to make the most of the time ahead of us and felt we had heard God correctly.

Major transition

We knew that getting married again would mean a major transition for both of us. We decided that I would move down to Bournemouth, mainly because my work was moveable, and Jilly's was not. This meant selling my bungalow in Yorkshire, and dispersing much of the furniture and belongings, a major physical task and not without its sadness. For Jilly, it meant adapting her home to make space for me and some of my cherished possessions. Jilly sees her clients at home, so with the help of church friends and Jilly's two sons, we built a garden office for me so that I could have somewhere to work and do my writing. This arrangement has worked well and helped enormously in our transition and adjustment.

We often say that for me the change has been mostly external and geographical, whereas for Jilly it has been internal and practical. For both of us, in different ways, it has been enormous and equally impactful. I have left my church of 30 years, my family and friends, familiar places and a known way of life. Jilly has given up her private space, welcomed me into her church and friendship circle, and coped with having a man around the house! Fortunately, we both have a good sense of humour, and have laughed a lot, which has helped us through some stressful times. We have both been committed to talking through issues as they arise and being open and honest with each other. Above all, we daily seek God's help and guidance for our marriage and seek to live with him as the centre of our relationship.

One thing that has taken us by surprise is how busy we have been. Bringing two established streams of life together takes time and attention. Our immediate family is dispersed in Yorkshire, Wales, Devon, and Australia, and we have felt building these relationships is a priority, which takes time and a lot of travelling. Furthermore, we need to get to know each other's friends, who are also scattered around the country. All this, plus the demands of our work, and the desire to be involved in our local church, mean that our days are enjoyable but very full.

Two are better than one

Something we have both appreciated is that we can lead retreats together. Jilly's amazing gift of counselling means she is a great listener, and people are instinctively drawn to her, so on retreat she will often be found giving quality time to individuals. She loves to lead people to encounter God in practical ways, such as Lectio Divina, a way of listening to God through scripture. Her gifts, combined with my teaching gift, make for a powerful combination. It often feels as if it was planned by God! We are learning from each other, and I have become more trauma aware because of our conversations about her work.

Much more could be said about this, and friends tease us that we should write a book together about second marriage, but that must wait for now. We need more experience first! Being married again, though, has given me a new lease of life. It has certainly been part of the adventure that God promised me, something I could never have imagined, but for which I am truly grateful. I am living in my spacious place!

Wherever he leads

One thing we are both conscious of is that every day is a gift from God. None of us know how many years we may have to live, so we must seize the day as the ancients said (*carpe diem*). Life is not permanent and cannot be taken for granted. In the last year I have lost four of my closest friends, each bereavement a reminder that I too am mortal. At the same time, we live with a sense that God still has a purpose for us, and we give ourselves fully to that. There is still much for us to learn, more to discover about our wonderful Saviour, and more adventurous paths to follow.

As long as God is leading us, with his help we will follow wherever he leads. Jesus has given us an example of what it means to be a true servant of God, delighting to do the Father's will, and with his grace we will follow in his steps (1 Peter 2:21).

Reflection 12:

DEEPER INTO LOVE

People often ask me if I am retired, and I find it an awkward question. I am now receiving my state pension, having reached retirement age some years ago, so I could technically retire and that would not be wrong. Yet I still have a call to serve, and although I am not as busy and carry less responsibility than before, I am still actively involved in ministry. So perhaps I am best described as semi-retired!

What occupies me most in my mid-70s is a hunger to know the love of God more deeply. Catholic theologians often describe the final stage of the Christian journey by the word 'union', an experience 'of complete oneness with God in which we find ourselves caught up in rapturous joy, adoration, praise, and a deep peace that passes all understanding'.[47] This is acknowledged to be a gift of grace and in no way the result of our human effort to know God more fully. It is a level of experience described by many of the ancient mystics like Bernard of Clairvaux (1090–1153), Julian of Norwich (1343–1416), Teresa of Avila (1515–82), St John of the Cross (1542–91), and Madam Guyon (1648–1717). It was the pursuit of God that dominated their lives, and in particular the desire to know his love as deeply as possible.

My own experience is nowhere near that of these worthies, but I am provoked by their writings and obvious delight in God not to settle for where I am in my relationship with God. Evangelical scholars would generally understand the term 'union' as our having been made 'one' with Christ at our conversion and united with him in his death and resurrection (Romans 6:8). This spiritual union is described by Jesus in John 15 where we are seen to be branches abiding in him who is the vine. From this perspective, union is not so much an experience as a position, a theological truth of great significance but not something to be known experientially. Yet I cannot help but think it can be, and should be, both. I believe that Jesus had in mind an intimate relationship, an intertwining of his life with ours, of which we are aware.

John and Charles Wesley, who spearheaded the great evangelical awakening in Britain during the 18th century, were never shy of experiencing God's love and encouraging others to do the same. For them, the love of God was like a mighty fire that burned within the heart. It was nothing less than the life of God in the soul, tangible and transformative. Charles penned a hymn in 1762 to express his belief:

> O thou who camest from above,
> the pure celestial fire to impart,
> kindle a flame of sacred love
> on the mean altar of my heart!

The holy love of God will set the soul on fire if we allow it to do so. Disciples are to be passionate and zealous, holy and pure. This is normal Christian experience, something for which we should earnestly pray. It will then energise and motivate all we do. Charles goes on to pray:

> There let it for thy glory burn
> with inextinguishable blaze,
> and trembling to its source return
> in humble love and fervent praise.

We are to be ablaze with the love of God, consumed by holy fire. This will never result in our being passive and withdrawn. The love of God is a force that always moves us outwards towards others and can never be contained or kept to oneself. To change the metaphor, it is a mighty river that flows into us, and then out from us, bringing life and blessing wherever it flows.

As we consider the needs of society in the western world, and the gap that exists between the church and most people, surely we must cry to God to revive us and pour out his love upon us in a way we have never seen before. Yes, many of us know for certain that we are loved by God, that we are his children and that he delights in us. We know the love of God to a certain degree – we might say to a comfortable degree. But do we know the love of God in all its fullness, in the reality that is holy love, a fire that burns and consumes? Maybe not.

If we are to seek the lost and welcome into our fellowship people who are broken and bruised, messed up by life in a fallen world, unfamiliar with church and gospel truths, we will need a radical dose of supernatural love. If our churches are to be home to people of different cultural and ethnic backgrounds, social strata, and generations, we will need to be free from any prejudices and judgementalism, able to see others through the eyes of divine love. If those whose lifestyles seem unusual to us – who don't dress like we do, share the values we have, or act in the same way as us – if such people are to come to Christ we will need a mighty baptism of heavenly love. Human love is insufficient for the challenges before us.

Jesus came into our world full of grace and truth. In him the fullness of God was made visible. Divine love appeared in human form, expressed through Jesus in mercy and compassion. The way he treated people is the way we are to treat people. Notice this, too – grace comes before truth, although both are equally important. We are to welcome people even before the truth has transformed them.

Mercy reflects the forbearance of God towards us, his choosing not to deal with us according to our sins but to tenderly forgive us and accept us. It expresses his kindness and understanding, his empathy towards frail and imperfect human beings. God's mercy is reflected in the cross of Christ, a direct reflection of his love for us. All believers have received mercy and are called to show mercy freely to others (Matthew 10:8).

Jesus always responded to a cry for mercy, as with blind Bartimaeus (Mark 10:48). He reminded the hard-hearted religious leaders of his day that God desires mercy not sacrifice (Matthew 12:3–8). Sometimes the rules need to be broken because human need is greater than upholding religious policies. It is legitimate to heal on the sabbath; it is right to take bread from the altar to feed the hungry. As James says, mercy should always triumph over judgement (James 2:13). Our first response should not be to judge, but to seek to understand. Mercy chooses not to be offended, and in love sees a hurting heart behind sinful actions.

Jesus was filled with compassion (Matthew 9:36, 14:14, 15:32, 20:34, Luke 15:20) and his heart went out in love to people in their need. He freely gave himself to others. This was more than a feeling of pity. It was a deep-seated emotion that moved him to action, a visceral experience that he felt deep within him, in his guts. It was the river of God's love moving out from him towards the sick, the hurting, the lost, the sad and lonely, the hungry and thirsty among the crowds that followed him.

The challenge for us is to allow God to soften our hearts. Yes, he has already taken out our heart of stone and given us a heart of flesh, that is, made us responsive and alive to himself (Ezekiel 36:26). But the reality is that our redeemed hearts can still be closed to the needs of others. As the apostle John says, we may see even our brothers and sisters in Christ with material needs, and yet despite feeling the prompting of the Spirit to help them, fail to share our resources with them (1 John 3:16–18). We can be cold, selfish, and protective of our own interests. We close our hearts. Only when we recognise and turn from our hardness of heart will God's love be able to flow freely from us. We need the fire of God to burn up the dross within us and create a greater capacity for self-giving love.

I wish I could say I was further down the path to a love-filled life than I am. There is still some way to go. Yet this is what I aspire to, and I think is a longing that is to be expected in the later years, when we can perhaps be more focused on the inner life and less absorbed in the whirl of activity that may have characterised our earlier years. Perhaps the words of John (the disciple whom Jesus loved), writing in his own later years, make an appropriate ending for this book, and a good summary of where the journey of discipleship is taking us:

> Dear friends, since God so loved us, we also ought to love one another. No one has ever seen God; but if we love one another, God lives in us and his love is made complete in us.
> 1 JOHN 4:11 12

Point of connection

The final stage of life is often described as 'elderhood', characteristically covering the 70s and 80s. Not all reach this period, while some live even longer. It is not simply a time of waiting for life to end. It can be, in God's economy, a special time of bearing fruit in keeping with the opportunities and limitations of this season.

Again, you may not have arrived here yet, but it is good to be aware of what it involves. If you are in this stage, then it will be helpful to reflect on what it holds for you.

- What do you think about the idea of retirement? Should we simply follow the patterns of society, or ask God to show us how to use these bonus years? What might that look like for you?

- What does a 'spirituality of ageing' suggest to you? How do we take our advancing years into account as we seek to continue our journey with God?

- It is easy to lose hope during these later years, which can be difficult in many ways. How can we remain positive and faith-filled? How can we strengthen our trust in God? How do you see this working out in my story?

- What do you think of the description of this stage as 'The Life of Love'? Is that an impossible ideal, or an aspiration to hold on to and seek after? What do you think it means to be 'one' with God?

- I speak about 'a baptism of love' that is needed in the church today. Why not pray for this for yourself, and your church?

- Consider the meaning of mercy and compassion as aspects of God's love that are most needed these days. Pray for them to be formed within you, and in your church community as a prelude to revival.

- Read again the words of the hymn by John Ernest Bode at the beginning of the book and make the prayer your own. What might be your next footsteps of faith?

You may like to keep working on your timeline, adding to it as further thoughts come to you. Is there anyone you would like to share it with? Why not consider writing your own story?

POSTSCRIPT

A letter to my younger self

Hi Tony

Congratulations! I see you have graduated now from London Bible College, are married to Evelyn, and are about to embark on your life as a missionary in the Asia. What an adventure awaits you!

I wonder if I might share some words of what I hope will be helpful advice from the perspective of your older self?

What jumps into my mind straight away is this: not everyone will like you! That may seem strange, and it may surprise you. After all, you are what the English call 'a decent sort of a chap' and you would never set out to offend anyone. Indeed, I know that harmony is important to you, and you are good at bringing diverse people together.

Even so, conflict will be part of your life, and this will be hard for you, but conflict is inevitable in ministry. It is not a sign of failure, or poor leadership, but of the difficulty involved in human relationships. It is how you respond to it that matters. You will need courage, and to be brave, but God will strengthen you when the time comes.

So, keep your eyes on Jesus. He is the one who called you, and he will never let you down. Other people will, and the church certainly will, but Jesus will never fail you or forsake you. Remember it is all about him. Make it your aim to stay close to him and to abide in him throughout your life. That way you will bear much fruit, and your life will be a blessing to many.

Remember, too, that life seldom works out exactly as we expect, so allow for the unexpected. The path marked out for you will have twists and turns, ups and downs, rough places as well as smooth. In all this, God is in control and is, in love, working out his perfect will for you, so trust him even when you are confused or disappointed.

His providence is always at work, weaving everything together for your ultimate good. You are in safe hands! One day you will be able to look back, as I am doing now, and see the beautiful tapestry he has woven throughout your life.

Above all, know this: it is not what we do that matters so much as who we become. It is all about becoming like Jesus and allowing his life to be expressed through yours. God is always working in us to achieve this, and through the years you will be very much aware of this inner transformation happening as you journey through life with him. Yield to what the Spirit is doing within you. It is much less painful that way!

One last thing. It is God's work, not ours. We are called to work together with him in a wonderful partnership where he is the senior partner. We are to work *with* God, not *for* God. This is a hard lesson to learn, and it will take you many years to grasp this fully, but you will get there. That will be the key to sustaining your ministry throughout the course of your life.

Tony, God will do more through you than you could ever imagine, so be careful to give the glory to him. Stay humble, stay amazed. A life of many adventures awaits you, and it will unfold gradually before you.

Do you remember the verse that Evelyn's auntie Helen wrote in the Bible she gave you just a few weeks ago? It said this: 'The one who calls you is faithful, and he will do it' (1 Thessalonians 5:24). That's it in a nutshell, and your life will be a visible testimony to that great truth.

Take heart, beloved child of God. Travel well. One step at a time, following Jesus all the way.

With love

Your much older self

A PRAYER

Lord, I offer myself to you again this day.
Take me as I am,
and use me for your glory.

I am weak and frail,
but you are strong
and your power works best
through human weakness.

I hold the light of your presence
and the treasure of your love
in the cracked, earthen vessel that is my life.

Shine your light through the cracks, Lord;
let your love seep out to those around me,
and its sweet aroma fill the air.

Fulfil every good purpose you have for me,
granting me grace to follow in your steps
until that day when you call me home
and the work you gave me to do
is complete.

Amen.

Appendix I:

LEADERSHIP DEVELOPMENT (SUMMARY)

– DR J. ROBERT CLINTON,
THE MAKING OF A LEADER

This appendix draws on *The Making of a Leader: Recognizing the lessons and stages of leadership development* (Nav Press, 1988) by Dr J. Robert Clinton, but has been written in Tony's own words and reflects his understanding of the material rather than direct excerpts from the book.

PHASE 1 – Sovereign foundations	PHASE 2 – Inner life growth	PHASE 3 – Ministry maturing
God working providentially in our lives to (a) prepare us and (b) save us.	Getting to know God, with godly character the issue.	Takes place over years.

PHASE 1 – Sovereign foundations

God working providentially in our lives to (a) prepare us and (b) save us.

This is a sovereign activity, for example:

1 How he made us
2 Family environment
3 Experiences that shape us
4 Training, background
5 The goal is conversion.

PHASE 2 – Inner life growth

Getting to know God, with godly character the issue.

Tests which reflect capacity for leadership and handling responsibility:

1 Integrity
2 Word (hearing God)
3 Obedience

Each test leads to an increased effectiveness.

4 Ministry task to illustrate faithfulness (Luke 16:10)

Moving from receiving to giving.

PHASE 3 – Ministry maturing

Takes place over years.

EARLY
Ministry challenge

MIDDLE
Concentrates on training

1 Ministry skills
2 Training experience
3 Giftedness discovery

LATER
Relational learning:

1 Authority, learning to submit
2 Relational insights
3 Ministry conflict
4 Leadership backlash

Learning discernment:

1 Spiritual warfare
2 Power items (prayer)
3 Faith challenges
4 Influence challenge
5 Ministry affirmation

N.B. Danger of plateauing and danger of burnout in this phase

PHASE 4 – Life maturity	PHASE 5 – Convergence	PHASE 6 – Afterglow/ Celebration
Shift from doing to being; ministry flowing out of being.	God leads us into a role which matches our gifts and experience so that ministry is maximised.	Not many reach this phase!
God's work in us gets stronger to develop greater maturity;		Era of recognition and wide influence. Storehouse of wisdom.
1 Isolation 2 Life crises 3 Conflict	Major question of guidance – trust, rest, and watch.	'Senior statesman or woman'
Successful ministry can't be based on gifts alone.	1 Major gift emerges 2 Philosophy of ministry 3 Training of others	
Spiritual authority comes as a by-product – the experience of God.		

Appendix II:

A ROAD MAP FOR THE SPIRITUAL JOURNEY

– JANET HAGBERG AND ROBERT GUELICH IN *THE CRITICAL JOURNEY*

This appendix draws on *The Critical Journey: Stages in the life of faith* (Sheffield Publishing Company, 1995) by Janet Hagberg and Robert Guelich, but has been written in Tony's own words and reflects his understanding of the material rather than direct excerpts from the book.

1 Recognition of God: this is the stage where we first become aware of God, either through a natural awareness of his existence that has always been with us, or through a sense of awe as we encounter him in the world he made, or through a sense of need for forgiveness or help with the problems of life. Faith is child-like and enthusiastic. 1 Thessalonians 1:9; Acts 8:6, 10:1–8, 13:12, 13:38–39, 14:15–18, 16:16–18, 16:30–34, 17:14–31.

2 The life of discipleship: now we get involved with a group of other believers, and begin to learn more about God from what we are taught. We learn what we have to do to become part of the group, and happily follow a leader we respect. We begin to identify our gifts and special contribution and may seek responsibility. Faith is secure and we carry a sense of rightness about what we believe. We are happy to be a good follower. Acts 2:42, 11:25–26, 14:21–23, 18:24–26; Hebrews 10:25; 2 Peter 3:18.

3 The productive life: faith is now expressed by working for God, and having found our unique place in the faith community we take on more responsibility, even coming into a leadership position. The emphasis is on productivity and success, and roles, titles, and recognition may be important. This may be a time when we take on further training and make decisions about 'full-time' ministry. Romans 12:3–8; 1 Corinthians 12:7–11; 1 Timothy 1:6, 2:15, 3:1, and 8; Acts 13:1–3; Ephesians 4:11–13; 2 Timothy 2:2.

4 The journey inward: here faith is rediscovering God. This may come about through a crisis of faith, and be accompanied by a loss of certainty. There may well be a search for a new direction, not necessarily answers. Having lived so much in the outer world we now give our attention to the inner world. God is released from the 'box' of our own understanding and tradition. Psalm 46:10; Matthew 11:28–30 (MSG); John 7:37–39.

○ The wall: although strictly part of stage 4, this experience is deemed so critical that it is treated separately. 'The wall' represents our will meeting God's will face-to-face. We decide anew whether we are willing to surrender and let God direct our lives. It is a pivotal moment in the journey, but often a place of mystery, and is different for everyone. All our defences and false identities are exposed, and the barriers we have made between ourselves and God begin to crumble. We may well resist the pain involved, but if we are willing to pass through 'The wall' it will become a time of healing, forgiveness, acceptance by God, and awareness of his unconditional love. Stillness and silence may become part of our journey. Galatians 2:20; John 15:4–5; 2 Corinthians 12:9–10.

5 The journey outward: faith is now surrendering to God more fully, and drawn closer to him through his unconditional love, we have a renewed sense of calling and ministry. Working from a place of rest within ourselves we are energised to focus now on the needs of others, but from a place of selfless love, not desire for success. John 15:8 and 16; 1 Corinthians 3:9, 15:10; Colossians 1:29.

6 The life of love: faith is now reflecting God as we begin to see Christ formed within us and live in total obedience to his will. Wisdom we have gained on the journey is used to help others, and we have a greater detachment from material things, and are freed from the stressful striving for position and power of earlier stages. There is a greater contentment about us and we are genuinely compassionate towards others. Ephesians 5:1–2; Philippians 4:12–13; 1 John 3:1 and 4:16–18.

Hagberg and Guelich are quick to point out that these stages are very fluid and that there is a lot of movement between them. They also describe how we can get stuck at any stage and they identify some of the factors that cause us to move on.

BOOKS BY TONY HORSFALL

All my books, apart from three, have been published by BRF Ministries, and they reflect the different stages of my journey with God. They will be helpful in fleshing out the themes that are covered in both the narrative and reflective sections of this book.

2001   *The Call to Intimacy* (Share the World.com)
2004   *Song of the Shepherd*
        Rhythms of Grace (Kingsway)
2006   *A Fruitful Life* (new edition 2019)
2008   *Mentoring for Spiritual Growth*
2010   *Working from a Place of Rest* (new edition 2023)
2012   *Rhythms of Grace* (BRF Ministries, new edition 2025)
2013   *Servant Ministry* (new edition 2019)
2015   *Deep Calls to Deep* (new edition 2021)
2016   *Spiritual Growth in a Time of Change* (new edition 2024)
2019   *Resilience in Life and Faith*
        Attentive to God (new edition 2025)
2020   *Mentoring Conversations*
        Love in a Time of Lockdown (self-published)
        Finding Refuge (self-published)
2022   *Grief Notes*
2023   *Knowing You, Jesus*
2026   *Footsteps of Faith*

NOTES

1 John R. W. Stott, *The Epistles of John*, Tyndale New Testament Commentaries (IVP, 1983), p. 96.

2 William Bridges, *Transitions: Making sense of life's changes* (Addison-Wesley, 1980), p. 122.

3 Dr J. Robert Clinton, *The Making of a Leader: Recognizing the lessons and stages of leadership development* (Nav Press, 1988), p. 13.

4 Janet Hagberg and Robert G. Guelich, *The Critical Journey: Stages in the life of faith* (Sheffield Publishing Company, 1995).

5 Randy Reese and Robert Loane, *Deep Mentoring: Guiding others on their leadership journey* (IVP, 2012), p. 79.

6 Krispin Mayfield, *Attached to God: A practical guide to deeper spiritual experience* (Zondervan, 2022), p. 7.

7 Reese and Loane, *Deep Mentoring*, p. 78.

8 David Benner, *The Gift of Being Yourself: The sacred call to self-discovery* (IVP, 2004), p. 16.

9 Keith Anderson, *Reading Your Life's Story: An invitation to spiritual mentoring* (IVP, 2016), p.18.

10 Reese and Loane, *Deep Mentoring*, p. 93.

11 Bill Hull, *The Complete Book of Discipleship: On being and making followers of Christ* (Nav Press, 2006), p. 24.

12 David Benner, *Surrender to Love: Discovering the heart of Christian spirituality* (IVP, 2003).

13 Benner, *Surrender to Love*, p. 66.

14 Hagberg and Guelich, *The Critical Journey*, p. 53.

15 Benner, *The Gift of Being Yourself*, p. 31.

16 Robert Mulholland, *Invitation to a Journey: A road map for spiritual formation* (IVP, 1993), p. 12.

17 Andrew Whitman, *When Jesus Met Hippies: The story and legacy of the Jesus People movement in the UK* (Malcolm Down Publishing, 2023).

18 Bill Hull, *The Christian Leader: Rehabilitating our addiction to secular leadership* (Zondervan, 2016), p. 107.

19 Shirley Lees, *Drunk before Dawn* (OMF Books, 1979) and Hudson Southwell, *Unchartered Waters* (Astana Publishing, 1999).

20 Clinton, *The Making of a Leader*, p. 107.

21 Marcus Honeysett, *Powerful Leaders?: When church leadership goes wrong and how to prevent it* (IVP, 2022), p. 3.

22 See, for example, the work of Living Leadership (**livingleadership. org**).

23 Quoted by C.J. Mahaney, *Humility: True greatness* (Multnomah, 2006), p. 29.

24 For an in-depth study of servanthood, see my own book *Servant Ministry: A portrait of Christ and a pattern for his followers* (BRF Ministries, 2019).

25 Clinton, *The Making of a Leader*, p. 163.

26 Reese and Loane, *Deep Mentoring*, p. 135.

27 Frederick Beuchner, *Listening to Your Life* (HarperSanFrancisco, 1992), p. 186.

28 Richard Foster, *Celebration of Discipline: The path to spiritual growth* (Hodder & Stoughton, 1980), p. 1.

29 Brennan Manning, *Abba's Child: The cry of the heart for intimate belonging* (NavPress, 1994), p. 59.

30 Alan Jamieson, *Chrysalis: The hidden transformation in the journey of faith* (Paternoster, 2007), p. 5.

31 Andrew Murray, *Abide in Christ* (James Nesbet, 1888), p. 140.

32 Marva J. Dawn, *Keeping the Sabbath Wholly: Ceasing, resting, embracing, feasting* (Eerdmans, 2001), p. 54.

33 Eugene Peterson, *The Pastor's Sabbath* (*Leadership* magazine, spring 1985), p. 53.

34 Anna L. Waring (1823–1910), 'In Heavenly Love Abiding'.

35 Henri Nouwen, *In the Name of Jesus: Reflections on Christian leadership* (DLT, 1989), p. 28.

36 Hagberg and Guelich, *The Critical Journey*, ch. 8.

37 Hagberg and Guelich, *The Critical Journey*, p. 136.

38 I am aware that the term 'influencer' is not always seen positively since it can suggest egotism and manipulation. It is used of those who create an online presence and by their personality and knowledge seek to influence the purchasing decisions of their followers. That is not how I use the term! I am thinking of helping and encouraging others in their growth in God by using the gifts, knowledge, and experience I have been given to help them make progress.

39 Mary and Charles Hippsley, *Reimagining the Landscape of Faith: Essential pathways for spiritual growth* (BRF Ministries, 2025), p. 228.
40 Mark Bradford, *The Space Between: The disruptive seasons we want to hide from, and why we need them* (BRF Ministries, 2021), p. 18.
41 Clinton, *The Making of a Leader*, p. 49.
42 Bill Webster, *When Someone You Care About Dies* (Centre for the Grief Journey, 2015), p. 3.
43 Jeff Manion, *The Land Between: Finding God in difficult transitions* (Zondervan, 2010), p. 19.
44 James Bryan Smith, *A Little Handbook of God's Love* (Hodder and Stoughton, 1995), p. 2, his italics.
45 Clinton, *The Making of a Leader*, p. 47.
46 Hagberg and Guelich, *The Critical Journey*, p. 152.
47 Mulholland, *Invitation to a Journey*, p. 97.

Reimagining the
Landscape of Faith
Essential pathways for spiritual growth

Every Christian carries a map, a mental image of their journey through life, created from their Christian tradition, their cultural background and their understanding of the Bible. Many Christians will also, at some point in their life, begin to question their map – causing them to ask, 'Is this all there is?' and 'How did I get here?' Mary and Charles Hippsley help us to identify our faith map, including the unexamined assumptions that underpin it. Then, drawing on a range of sources of wisdom including personal experience, they gently encourage us to allow God to expand our map when we find that our faith doesn't match up with the reality of life. They aim to equip the reader to navigate their journey towards maturity by exploring new paths and landscapes of faith.

Reimagining the Landscape of Faith
Essential pathways for spiritual growth
Mary and Charles Hippsley
978 1 80039 271 7 £12.99

brfresources.org.uk

Where do we turn when our world is falling apart? It takes courage to hope; to stand in our confusion and grief and still to believe that 'God is not helpless among the ruins'. Guided by Habakkuk and his prophetic landmarks, we are drawn on a reflective journey through the tangled landscape of bewildered faith, through places of wrestling and waiting, and on into the growth space of deepened trust and transformation. As you read, discover for yourself the value and practice of honest prayer, of surrender, of silence and listening, and of irrepressible hoping.

God Among the Ruins
Trust and transformation in difficult times
Mags Duggan
978 0 85746 575 7 £8.99

brfresources.org.uk

Ministries

Inspiring people of all ages to grow in Christian faith

BRF Ministries is the
home of Anna Chaplaincy,
BRF Resources, Messy Church
and Parenting for Faith

As a charity, our work would not be possible without
fundraising and gifts in wills.
To find out more and to donate,
visit brf.org.uk/give or call +44 (0)1865 319700

Registered with
FUNDRAISING
REGULATOR